S0-BAT-719

Child Abuse: An Interdisciplinary Analysis

Child Abuse: An Interdisciplinary Analysis

Ross D. Parke and Candace Whitmer Collmer

The University of Chicago Press
Chicago and London

Ross D. Parke, formerly of Fels Research Institute, is presently professor of psychology and chairman of the Division of Developmental Psychology at the University of Illinois, and associate editor of *Child Development*.

Candace Whitmer Collmer, formerly of Fels Research Institute, is presently working toward a Ph.D. degree in botany at Cornell University.

The University of Chicago Press, Chicago 60637
The University of Chicago Press, Ltd., London

© 1975 by The University of Chicago
All rights reserved. Published 1975
Printed in the United States of America

International Standard Book Number: 0-226-33165-2
Library of Congress Catalog Card Number: 75-26043

This work originally appeared as Chapter 9 of
Review of Child Development Research, Volume 5
(1975), edited by E. Mavis Hetherington and
published under the auspices of *Child Development*
and the Society for Research in Child Development.

Contents

I. INTRODUCTION

Few problems in recent times have aroused the concern of American society to the extent of child abuse. It is a shocking fact that many thousands of children are beaten, sexually molested, and neglected annually in the United States. The purpose of this paper is to provide a review and analysis of the problem of physical abuse of children. Attention will be paid to an evaluation of alternative theoretical models that have been proposed to account for child abuse. Finally, treatment programs aimed at reducing the incidence of abuse will be examined. "Child abuse," as a term, can cover many different forms of maltreatment of children. This review is restricted to the use of excessive physical force by parents usually in the home environment. The use of extreme forms of physical discipline by school teachers and other school authorities is outside the scope of this review. Similarly, sexual abuse of children by adults will not be considered in this chapter.

II. TOWARD A DEFINITION OF CHILD ABUSE

A variety of definitions of child abuse have been offered and none is free of ambiguities. There are parallels between attempts at defining child abuse and defining other types of social behavior such as aggression. There are two principal approaches to the definition of physical abuse. First, abuse can be defined in terms of outcomes, which serves to focus attention on the injuries. From this perspective, abuse would be defined as "behavior that results in injury of another individual." The advantage of this type of definition is that certain objectively quantifiable levels of injury could be established as standards for invoking the label of child abuse and inferences about the injuring agent's intent or motives would be minimized. Buss (1961) has advocated this approach in

The chapter was prepared with the support of National Science Foundation grant SOC72-05220 A03 to Ross D. Parke. Thanks to a number of individuals for critical comments and suggestions on earlier drafts of this chapter, including Frank Falkner, E. Mavis Hetherington, Robert D. Kavanaugh, C. Henry Kempe, Gerald R. Patterson, John B. Reid, Douglas B. Sawin, Suzanne K. Steinmetz, and Murray A. Straus. A special note of appreciation to the members of the 1974 Summer Seminar on Child Abuse at the Institute of Child Development, University of Minnesota, who contributed significantly to the clarification of the conceptual foundations of this chapter. The group included Susan Adelson, Pauline Banford, Wyndol Furman, Royal G. Grueneich, Michael C. Lougee, Janice R. Mokros, and Brian E. Vaughn. Finally, thanks to Francess Hall and Cathy Pinslow for their able assistance in preparation of the manuscript.

defining aggressive behavior. However, there are serious limitations to this type of definition. In this case, children receiving accidental injuries would be grouped with those who were victims of intentionally inflicted injuries. Consider the following example: parent A in a moment of anger pushes child A against a table corner injuring his head, while parent B in the course of a friendly game pushes child B who falls and injures his head. Both children are injured, and by an objective definition both parents would be described as abusive. But it is obvious that we need a definition that excludes accidental occurrences.

The second approach to definition of physical abuse recognizes the need to include the concept of intentionality. Kempe and Helfer (1972) give recognition to the concept of intentionality in their definition of abuse: ". . . any child who received nonaccidental physical injury (or injuries) as a result of acts (or omissions) on the part of his parents or guardians" (p. 1). While this does eliminate accidental occurrences of injury, many would object to this definition because of the difficulties encountered by the use of the concept of intentionality. The introduction of intent into the definition raises a serious problem, since intent is not part of the observable behavior but can most often be inferred from antecendent conditions and context. This type of definition involves more than an observable act or sequence of behavior which can be reliably measured, since the observer must also make judgments or inferences concerning the actor's intention. Neither laymen nor professionals are very accurate in judging another person's intentions, and thus problems of the reliability and validity of judgments of intent often arise.

A third approach to defining child abuse recognizes that physical abuse is not a set of behaviors but, rather, a culturally determined label which is applied to behavior and injury patterns as an outcome of a social judgment on the part of the observer (Walters & Parke 1964). Intention is merely one criterion that we typically employ in deciding whether an interpersonal exchange between an adult caretaker and a child is abusive. In making this judgment, an observer takes into account a variety of factors, including the antecedents of the response, the form and intensity of the response, the extent of the injury, and the role and status of the agent and victim of the behavior. In short, an injury will be labeled abuse in one situation or in one child or in one social class, and the same injury may not be judged abuse in another situation, child, or social class. For example, is an injury incurred by a child from a poor family more likely to be labeled abuse than a similar injury incurred by a child from a middle-class family? Even an objective definition of child abuse in terms of injuries must include standards concerning the severity of outcome which, in turn, are culturally defined. From this viewpoint, the definition of child abuse will vary with social class and the cultural background of the defining individual. Child abuse is a community-defined phenomenon, which must be viewed in the context of community norms and standards governing the appropriate conduct of adults in their interactions with their own and others' children. To date, insufficient attention has been paid to the development of an empirically derived set of standards based on community consensus concerning the rights of children and parents. An adequate definition of child abuse must give explicit recognition to the community-defined bases of the phenomenon.

To illustrate the confusion that may arise if a definition deviates from commonly accepted community standards of appropriate parental behavior, consider the definition offered by Gil in "Violence against Children": "Physical abuse of children is the intentional, nonaccidental use of force, on the part of a parent or other caretaker interacting with a child in his care aimed at hurting, injuring or destroying that child" (Gil 1970, p. 6). There are serious conceptual problems with Gil's definition, which flow in part from a failure to distinguish between actual community attitudes toward the use of physical punishment as a technique of discipline and one's own ideological views concerning the acceptability of these disciplinary techniques. Included in this definition are "all uses of physical force aimed at hurting, injuring or destroying a child irrespective of the degree of seriousness of the act and/or the outcome" (Gil 1970, p. 6). However, is it useful to include all parents who use physical force in the form of physical punishment in a definition of abuse? It is not merely from the viewpoint of community standards that this approach can be questioned. Consider the following estimates: Stark and McEvoy (1970) report that 93% of parents surveyed use physical punishment although some use it only rarely and only on young children. In contrast, Gil estimates that approximately 2.3%–3.7% of the population are subject to abuse. Therefore, it is questionable whether a definition which includes over 90% of the population is sufficiently discriminating to be useful.

A final problem of definition flows from the assumption that physical abuse is a single phenomenon; in fact, as we will note in the later sections, there are many types of physical abuse—whether defined in terms of the situations that elicit abuse, or in terms of the parents who abuse, or in terms of the types of injuries and victims.

For purposes of this review a modification of the Kempe-Helfer definition of child abuse will be employed: any child who receives nonaccidental physical injury (or injuries) as a result of acts (or omissions) on the part of his parents or guardians that violate the community standards concerning the treatment of children.

III. SCOPE OF THE PROBLEM

A. RATE OF INCIDENCE

At present the exact scope of child abuse is unknown. However, there are a number of statistics that help define the magnitude of the problem. There are two principal sources of data: hospital and community agency reports and a recent national survey (Gil 1970). Kempe (1971) estimated that there were as many as six incidents of physical abuse per 1,000 births in the United States. And, more recently, Kempe (1973) estimates that approximately 60,000 children were seriously abused during 1972. Fontana (1973) suggests that the annual rate is 1.5 million cases of child abuse. However, to illustrate the seriousness of the reporting problem— since the inception of a central registry in New York in 1966, the local rate of abused children has increased 549%. Similarly, in 1968, there were 11,000 cases of child abuse filed in all state registries, but by 1972 the number doubled. Whether this increase in reported cases of child abuse reflects a real increase in the problem is questionable. Apparent increases in child abuse rates may, in part, be due to shifts in public and professional awareness and knowledge of child abuse in conjunction with more stringent reporting laws and better legal protection for persons who report cases of abuse.

In light of the potential error in utilizing agency estimates, other techniques for estimating the incidence of child abuse have been employed. Another approach to the incidence problem comes from Gil (1970), who conducted a national survey to determine public awareness of child abuse. Gil assumed that members of the community know of cases of child abuse, even though these cases are never reported to professional authorities or at least never appear in the incidence statistics. In conjunction with the National Opinion Research Center, Gil surveyed a sample of 1,520 people which represented the total noninstitutionalized population of the United States over 21 years old or under 21 and married. They were asked "whether they personally knew families involved in incidents of child abuse resulting in physical injury during the prior 12 months." Forty-five individuals or 3% of the sample of 1,520 people reported such knowledge of 48 different incidents. Extrapolating from this outcome to the total U. S. population of 110 million and allowing for a margin of error, Gil estimated that there were between 2.53 and 4.07 million adults throughout the United States who personally knew families involved in incidents of child abuse during the preceding year. These figures, as Gil notes, must be interpreted cautiously, since there may be some overlap in the cases of abuse known to different respondents. More recently, Light (1973) has offered a more conservative estimate of physical abuse by applying a series of corrective assumptions to Gil's original data. By assuming that each respondent in the survey knew more than one family and were differentially acquainted with other families, and by further adjustment for the average number of abused children per family (1.6), Light estimates that there are approximately 500,000 abused children in the United States. In any case, the numbers of abused children are sufficiently large to justify a major effort to determine the causes of this phenomenon. These figures should not imply that child abuse is a peculiarly American phenomenon. Other English-speaking countries, such as Canada (Harrison 1968; Van Stolk 1972), Australia (Committee Report 1967), and Great Britain (Skinner & Castle 1969), report incidents of child abuse. In Britain, estimates are that, of 500,000 infants born, 3,000 will be seriously injured or deprived. Similarly, non-English-speaking countries, such as Germany, report similar problems (Torgerson 1973, cited by Bellak & Antell 1974).

B. SOURCES OF UNRELIABILITY IN ABUSE ESTIMATES

Most approximations of the incidence of child abuse in the United States probably underestimate the actual rate of occurrence. What are the reasons for the vast discrepancy between actual reported figures of child abuse and the frequencies reported by Gil's interviewees concerning their knowledge of abuse cases? There are a number of possible reasons. First, parents may simply not take the child or infant for medical attention. Second, parents who are repeated abusers may shift hospitals and/or physicians in order to reduce the likelihood that their child's repeated injuries will form the basis for classification as abuse, but instead be seen as accidents. Third, the types of injuries that are inflicted may sometimes not easily be detected. Fourth, the physician may fail to report the case to a central registry and so no record is available. (Becker [1973; cited by Light 1973] noted that of 3,000 reported cases of child abuse collected from New York City's Central Registry only eight were reported by physicians). Fifth, definitions of abuse vary across geographic areas and across public health personnel, and the reported instances of abuse vary from state to state. Another reason may stem from recognition of our potential for abuse, which is confirmed by the results of Gil's survey (1970). Fifty-eight percent of Gil's sample assumed that "almost anybody could at some time injure a child in his care," while over 22% thought that they "could at some time injure a child." Even more striking is the finding that nearly 16% of the interviewed admitted coming very close to injuring a child in their care. This recognition of our vulnerability may lead to a "tacit agreement among us not to meddle in each other's private matters" (Zalba 1971, p. 61). In addition, as Zalba notes, there is a prevailing strong conception of children as property, and some reluctance to intervene may flow from this view of parental rights in the treatment of children.

In light of the fact that large numbers of abused children go undetected, suggestions to improve our identification of abused children have been offered. Kempe (1973) has suggested that the United States develop a system of national health visitors, similar to the visitor system in operation in Aberdeen, Scotland.

> We suggest that a health visitor call at intervals during the first months of life upon each young family and that she become, as it were, the guardian who would see to it that each infant is receiving his basic health rights. . . . It is my view that the concept of the utilization of health visitors would be widely accepted in this country. Health visitors need not have nursing training, and intelligent, successful mothers and fathers could be readily prepared for this task at little cost. . . . In those areas where it is not practical to have health visitors health stations could be established in neighborhood fire houses. [Kempe; cited by Light 1973, p. 568]

While this may, in fact, be an economically feasible means of improving our detection rates, there are some serious problems with large-scale screening programs that may outweigh the benefits. Light (1973), in a thoughtful discussion of this issue, raises three general potential difficulties that merit consideration. Evaluation of the massive screening must be viewed in the context of the incidence of abuse. If a very high proportion of children were abused, then the expense, inconvenience, and even minimal harm incurred in the detection process could be easily justified. However, abuse, fortunately, has a low base rate and, therefore, the costs to the large majority of nonabused children must be weighed against the cost of the nondetection of a small number of abused children. Light illustrates this problem by a consideration of the implications of using X-ray techniques as standard diagnostic procedures to detect abuse. "If one child in a hundred is really abused, then even if this case were detected via x-ray, 99 would be needlessly exposed to x-ray diagnosis. . . . It is not clear that the benefit of detecting the one case outweighs the cost of cumulative exposure of the other ninety-nine children" (Light 1973, p. 568).

Second, the relative incidence of abuse in contrast to the incidence of other health problems must be considered. Is the cost of abuse detection in the best overall interests of children? There may be other problems that are more serious, such as nutrition. On the other hand, there is no reason to restrict a large-scale screening examination to the detection of only one type of problem.

The final problem is the most serious one, namely, the error rate in detection. Two types are possible: false negatives, whereby the test fails to detect an abused child, and false positives, whereby the test suggests that a child is abused when this is not the case. Light (1973) empirically demonstrated the fact that with a low base rate event, such as child abuse, even small margins of error will result in high levels of false positives. Even in a situation where an abused child is detected 90% of the time and nonabuse is correctly detected 95% of the time, 85% of the parents who are accused of abuse would be falsely accused. This possibility of false detection does not necessarily, of course, undermine the usefulness of a national health examiniation for detection of abuse. However, diagnostic personnel require excellent training in order to minimize detection error. Light recommends an alternative approach that will reduce some of the detection error—a multiple-stage checking procedure. "At the first stage, where large numbers of children are examined, the primary focus should be on avoiding false negatives, missing real cases of abuse. But, subsequent stages should steadily work towards winnowing out questionable cases, leaving the focus at the final stage on avoiding false positives, and the resulting false accusation of parents" (Light 1973, p. 571). A final consideration, of course, is the type of intervention that would follow from the detection. If the intervention involved advice and aid in child care, and increasing the family's awareness of community resources and services, without any direct accusation, the false detection would not be so serious. More intrusive intervention, however, raises serious questions concerning the privacy rights of parents.

IV. Approaches to Understanding Child Abuse

There have been three approaches to understanding child abuse. The first and most predominant model derives from psychiatric analyses of the abusing parent. The distinctive feature of this approach is the focus on the parent as the principal cause of the abuse; it is assumed that the abusive parents have a set of personality characteristics that distinguish them from other parents. In addition, there is the implicit assumption that abusive parents are abnormal or "sick" and therefore require extensive psychiatric treatment in order to overcome their "illness." A second model of child abuse is sociological. In this case the causal focus shifts from the parent to the social environment. Abuse is assumed to be a result of the stress and frustration encountered by parents in their daily attempts to cope with their social environment. From this viewpoint, alleviation of the stress encountered, particularly by lower-class parents, is the main recommendation for the reduction of abuse. A third approach is a social-situational model of child abuse. This shares with the sociological model the common assumption that child abuse can be best understood by an examination of external environmental events that impinge on families. The level of analysis is, however, different. This approach assumes that a detailed exploration of the patterns of interaction between family members will be useful. In this model, the child as an active participant and elicitor of abuse is given full recognition. Specification of the events that elicit and maintain the use of physically punitive tactics in interpersonal control in the family context and the isolation of the specific circumstances under which abusive incidents occur are the aims of this type of analysis. In the following sections, the main supporting data for each of these three approaches will be discussed as well as the unique treatment implications of each model.

A. PSYCHIATRIC MODEL OF CHILD ABUSE

There are a variety of approaches subsumed under the psychiatric model. First, abusive parents may be classified into traditional psychiatric diagnostic categories such as schizophrenia or manic-depressive psychosis. In this case, the abusive behavior is viewed as a manifestation of a broader underlying psychosis. Although some psychotic individuals are responsible for child abuse, estimates indicate that less than 10% of the child-abusive adults can be classified as mentally ill (Kempe 1973). In fact, as Spinetta and Rigler (1972) note:

There has been an evolution in thinking regarding the presence of a frank psychosis in the abusing parent. Woolley and Evans (1955) and Miller (1959) posited a high incidence of neurotic or psychotic behavior as a strong etiological factor in child abuse. Cochrane (1965), Greengard (1964), Platou, Lennox and Beasley (1964) and Simpson (1967, 1968) concurred. Adelson (1961) and Kaufman (1962) considered only the most violent and abusive parents as having schizophrenic personalities. Kempe et al. (1962), allowing that direct murder of children betrayed a frank psychosis on the part of the parent, found that most of the abusing parents, though lacking in impulse control, were not severely psychotic. By the end of the decade, the literature seemed to support the view that only a few of the abusing parents showed severe psychotic tendencies (Fleming, 1967; Laupus, 1966; Steele & Pollock, 1968; Wasserman, 1967). [Spinetta & Rigler 1972, p. 299]

And the trend has continued. Blumberg (1974) recently noted that viewing the abusive parent as psychotic was a misconception of a psychiatric analysis of child abusing. "Psychosis is very rarely a factor in child abuse. The number of children harmed or killed by schizophrenic parents is only a very small fraction of the total" (Blumberg 1974, p. 22).

1. Personality Characteristics of Abusive Parents

Although psychiatric classification of abusive parents is on the wane, attempting to discover distinctive personality characteristics is still a fashionable strategy. Typically, this involves the listing of personality traits that characterize abusive parents derived either from clinical interviews and diagnosis or from a set of standardized test instruments.

The most systematic and well-controlled study of personality attributes of child-abusing mothers has been reported by Melnick and Hurley (1969). Using largely lower-class black mothers, they compared groups of 10 abusive and 10 control mothers, matched for age, social class, and education, on 18 personality variables. The tests used in the study were the California Test of Personality (CTP), the Family Concept Inventory (FCI), the Manifest Rejection Scale (index of general harshness of parental disciplinary policies), and 12 TAT cards. The abusing mothers revealed lower self-esteem (CTP), less family satisfaction (FCI), a higher pathogenic index (TAT), less need to give nurturance (TAT), higher frustration of need dependence (TAT), and a less openly rejectant stance toward children.

Even this well-controlled study has the serious limitation of being based on a small and highly select sample (lower-class black mothers), and the generalizability of these findings is questionable. Whether similar traits are applicable to fathers, middle-class parents, or other ethnic groups is unknown. Moreover, the lack of differences was also striking: the two groups of mothers did not differ on 12 of the 18 personality dimensions.

Various other investigators have offered their own descriptions of abusing parents ranging from rigid and domineering (Johnson & Morse 1968), to impulsive, immature, self-centered, and hypersensitive (Kempe et al. 1962). However, there has been little success in constructing a consistent set of personality traits. After an extensive analysis of the literature on personality characteristics, Spinetta and Rigler (1972) concluded that "a review of opinions on parental personality and motivational variables leads to a conglomerate picture. While the authors generally agree that there is a defect in the abusing parent's personality that allows aggressive impulses to be expressed too freely (Kempe et al. 1962; Steele & Pollock 1968; Wasserman 1967), disagreement comes in describing the source of the aggressive impulses" (Spinetta & Rigler 1972, p. 299). In another recent review, Gelles (1973) found that, of 19 traits noted by various investigators, there was agreement by two or more authors on only four traits, with the remaining 15 characteristics being unique to one particular author.

Although specific traits may be difficult to isolate, other investigators have attempted to discover clusters of traits that might characterize the abusive parent more adequately then the single-trait approach (Delsordo 1963; Merrill 1962; Zalba 1967). At present, there has been no attempt to empirically validate or cross-validate these typologies and so their usefulness in detecting high-risk parents *or* in economically representing and organizing findings from other investigations of personality traits remains to be determined.

A variety of other problems limit the usefulness of currently available studies of personality characteristics. With a few exceptions (e.g., Melnick & Hurley 1969), there are no comparison groups of nonabusers that are drawn either from other types of clinical populations or from nonclinical normal populations. Consequently, it is impossible to assess whether these personality traits are unique to child-abusing adults. Even psychiatric advocates such as Steele and Pollock comment, "Such adjectives are essentially appropriate when applied to those who abuse children, yet these qualities are so prevalent among people in general that they add little specific understanding" (Steele & Pollock 1968, p. 109). Second, the samples of abusive individuals employed in developing the lists of traits may be unique. "Most of the data are gathered from cases that medical or psychiatric practitioners have at hand. Thus, the sample cannot be considered truly representative of child abusers since many or most are not seen in clinics" (Gelles 1973, p. 614). These criticisms do not imply that more carefully conducted studies may not reveal specific and unique personality traits that can be useful in the screening and detection of potential child-abusing adults. However, in light of the accumulating evidence of the limited relationship between personality traits and actual behavior (Mischel 1968, 1973), this does not appear to be a very fruitful approach.

One final comment: the only general conclusion that Spinetta and Rigler (1972) were able to draw was that "a general defect in character—from whatever source—is present in the abusing parent allowing aggressive impulses to be expressed too freely" (1972, pp. 300–301). This kind of tautological explanation is, unfortunately, too often characteristic of a personality approach. Since nearly all research on child abuse is ex post facto, one wonders about the usefulness of re-describing the abusive parent as being low in aggression control. That descriptive characterization should be the starting point in attempting to understand the behavior and is not, in any sense, an explanation. Re-labeling is not a substitute for adequate explanation.

2. Child-rearing Histories of Abusing Parents

Although there is only limited agreement on the particular personality characteristics of abusive parents, there is more consensus on the distinctive child-rearing attitudes of abusing parents. It has been reported by a wide range of investigators that abusing parents were very frequently abused and neglected as children (Curtis 1963; Kempe et al. 1962; Steele & Pollack 1968; cf. Spinetta & Rigler 1972 for an extensive summary of this literature). Moreover, as children they may have experienced more than just exposure to physically abusive patterns. Perhaps more important as a factor in the occurrence of their own abusive behavior later was their childhood deprivation of basic mothering. Steele and Pollock (1968), in their classic psychiatric examination of abusive parents, view "the lack of mothering," defined as "a lack of the deep sense of being cared for and cared about from the beginning of one's life," as "a most basic factor in the genesis of parental abuse" (p. 112). Not only have abusive parents learned patterns of aggressive behavior as children, but also they have experienced a "pattern of demand, criticism, and disregard designed to suit the mother and leave the [child] out" (p. 112). It is assumed that this pattern of demanding, aggressive behavior experienced in childhood leads to abusive parental behavior in adulthood. A number of other studies generally confirm the intergenerational consistency of abuse; it is clear that the parent's own child-rearing history is an important determinant of abuse. In a later section, the manner in which rearing with physically punitive tactics contributes to parental abusive behavior will be discussed in more detail.

3. Summary

In this section, the psychiatric approach to child abuse was outlined. This approach emphasizes the parent as the principal cause of abuse and assumes that there are personality characteristics that distinguish abusive parents. Implicit in this approach is the assumption that abusive parents are abnormal or ill. The failure to identify distinctive personality factors casts some doubt on the utility of the psychiatric approach. Finally, the child-rearing histories of abusive parents revealed a consistent picture of aggressive, physically punitive childhood experiences.

B. SOCIOLOGICAL MODEL OF CHILD ABUSE

From a sociological perspective, the focus is not on individual differences as in the psychiatric model but on the social values and social organization of the culture, the community, and the family as contributors to child abuse. It is assumed that an examination of the social-cultural context in which abuse occurs offers a useful perspective for understanding child abuse.

First, it is assumed that child abuse can be understood by an examination of "the society's basic social philosophy and value premises" (Gil 1974, p. 12) and more specifically by an examination of the prevailing cultural attitudes toward violence and the use of physical force as a form of control in interpersonal interactions. Second, it is assumed that position of the family in the social-economic hierarchy is an important key to understanding child abuse. Underlying the assumption is a cumulative stress model, which suggests that the degree of stress and frustration encountered by individuals in different positions in the social structure is a determinant of abuse. Finally, it is assumed that the structure and organization of the family and the family relationship to sources of community support are relevant determinants of child abuse. In this section, a critical examination of each of these three facets of the sociological model are presented.

1. The Cultural Attitude to Violence as a Contributor to Child Abuse

It has been proposed that the level of child abuse in American society is, in part, due to our cultural sanctioning of physical force for resolving interpersonal conflict (Gil 1970). To assess the accuracy of this proposal, first, let us examine the level of violence in American society (Palmer 1972; Pinkney 1972). Comparisons of our rate of violent murder with other countries is instructive. In the United States there were nearly 20,000 murders known to the police in 1972 or a rate of 8.9 per 100,000 inhabitants (Kelley 1973), whereas the rate is only one-tenth as high in England (Geis & Monahan 1975). Similarly, the assault-and-battery rate for Canada in 1968 was 28.6 per 100,000, while the U. S. rate was 141 per 100,000 (Steinmetz 1974a). Similarly, cross-cultural comparisons of the level of television violence indicate that the United States is, again, higher than other countries such as Sweden, Israel, or Britain. (Liebert, Neale, & Davidson 1973). In a careful analysis of the content of TV programs over a 5-year period, Gerbner (1972) found that over 75% of the programs contained violence. Elsewhere in this volume, Stein and Freidrich summarize the effects of this type of exposure: both behavior and attitudes are shaped by this type of TV programming. In fact, there is a consistently presented moral lesson that children and adults are repeatedly exposed to, namely, that violence is an appropriate means for resolving conflict. Moreover, there are other forms of institutionalized violence that are commonly executed by corporate and government officials (such as failures to enforce pollution standards and permitting dangerous drugs to be profitably marketed) (see Geis & Monahan 1975 for a fuller discussion of these subtler forms of violence).

There is other evidence that suggests that the levels of violence in a society are reflected in the levels of violence in the family. More generally, the conflict resolution strategies that are predominant at a societal level appear to be mirrored in family interaction patterns. First, let us examine the cross-cultural data. Bellak and Antell (1974), in a comparison of German, Italian, and Danish cities, found that the higher suicide and homicide rates corresponded to an equally higher level of both parental and child aggression. Similarly, Steinmetz (1974a) in a U. S.-Canada comparison found lower levels of intrafamilial aggression in Canada, where the levels of criminal aggressive activity are also lower.

Closer examination of familial violence reveals striking degrees of interrelationship among marital conflict tactics, disciplinary techniques, and the methods employed by children in settling sibling conflicts. Steinmetz (1974b) found that families who use verbal and physically aggressive tactics for resolution of husband-wife disputes tend to use similar types of techniques in disciplining their children; the children, in turn, tend to duplicate these tactics in their sib/sib relationships.

In light of these replicated patterns of violence across societal, media, and familial levels, it is not surprising that physical punishment is a widely used disciplinary and child-rearing technique in American society. Stark and McEvoy (1970) report that 93% of all parents use physical punishment, although some use it only rarely and only on young children. In fact, one investigation (Korsch et al. 1965) revealed that in their sample of 100 Los Angeles mothers one-quarter of the mothers were spanking their infants in the first 6 months of life and nearly half were spanking their infants by the end of the first year. However, other studies (Steinmetz 1974c; Straus 1971) report that physical punishment is not restricted to young children. For example, Straus found that 52.3% of the subjects in his adolescent sample had experienced actual or threatened physical punishment during their last year of high school. Further, professional groups, as well as parents, advocate the use of physical punishment. Viano (1974) found that two-thirds of the educators, police, and clergy questioned condoned physical discipline in the form of hand-administered spanking, while over 10% of the police and clergy condoned spanking children for disciplinary purposes with belts, straps, and brushes! Finally, recent studies indicate that physical punishment as a disciplinary technique is used at all social class levels (Erlanger 1974), which is, of course, contrary to earlier reports of social class differences in punitiveness (Bronfenbrenner 1958). In general, these social class differences in punitiveness have been overstated.

Is the widespread use of physical punishment as a child-rearing technique in American society a factor in the level of child abuse? Gil argues the case as follows: "A key element to understanding child abuse of children in the United States seems to be that the context of child rearing does not exclude the use of physical force toward children by parents and others responsible for their socialization. Rather, American culture encourages in subtle and at times not so subtle ways the use of 'a certain measure' of physical force in rearing children" (Gil 1970, p. 134).

Some support for this viewpoint comes from studies of other cultures where there is no sanctioning of physical punishment as a child-rearing tactic. Recent visitors to China (Sidel 1972; Stevenson 1974) report only rare use of physical punishment, little aggression among children, and no incidents of child abuse. More direct evidence comes from comparisons of the child-rearing tactics used by Taiwan parents in controlling their 4–5-year-old children with disciplinary practices of white American parents (Niem & Collard 1971). The Chinese parents reported using any form of physical punishment less than half as often as American parents and spankings were only one-quarter as frequent among the Chinese families. Alternatively, the Chinese families used love-oriented discipline twice as often as American parents. While a number of factors may account for these findings, temperament differences indicating the greater soothability and less emotional lability among Chinese newborns may, in fact, make these children less troublesome (Freedman & Freedman 1969). Goode (1971) has noted a similar situation in Japan, where physical punishment is not a common disciplinary tactic and child abuse is infrequent. Similarly, parents in a number of other cultures where there are few reports of child abuse such as the Arapesh (Mead 1935) and the Tahitians (Levy 1969) raise their children without physical punishment.

In summary, these cross-cultural examples suggest that variations in the cultural level of violence are reflected in family violence and particularly in the prevalence of physical punishment as a child-rearing technique. Whether these variations in disciplinary practices are, in fact, responsible for different levels of child abuse is left unanswered. However, the ways in which physical punitiveness *can* lead to child abuse will be examined in more detail in a later section—the social-situational analysis of child abuse.

Next we shift from a cultural level of analysis to an examination of the relationship between the individual's position in the social hierarchy and child abuse.

2. Social Stress, Social Class, and Child Abuse

One of the assumptions underlying the sociological model of child abuse is that stress and frustration elicit abusive behavior; second, it is assumed that the degrees of stress are related to the social status of the individual, with lower socioeconomic groups experiencing greater amounts of environmental stress. To test these assumptions, it is necessary to examine the relationship between social class and child abuse. First, child abuse is not restricted to a single socioeconomic class in particular; it is not merely a lower-class phenomenon. It is one of the myths of a middle-class social science that intrafamily violence is concentrated in the lower socioeconomic groups (Steinmetz & Strauss 1974).

A number of investigators have reported cases of child abuse in both middle- and upper-class families (Allen, Ten Bensel, & Raile 1968; Boardman 1962; Bryant et al. 1963; de Francis 1963; Gillespie 1965; Helfer & Kempe 1968, 1974; Helfer & Pollock 1968; Laury 1970; Nurse 1964; Steele & Pollock 1968; Ten Bensel & Raile 1963; Young 1964).

However, the results of the recent Gil survey (1970) have given renewed impetus to a class-linked view of child abuse. Since this study has been very influential, it is important to examine this investigation critically. In 1967 and 1968, Gil executed a nationwide survey of child abusers in order to provide a comprehensive demographic sketch of child-abusing adults and their victims. To increase the accuracy of his survey, standardized reporting forms were developed for use by central registries of child abuse in each state. Approximately 6,000 cases were studied in 1967 and a new and slightly larger sample was examined in 1968. Gil analyzed detailed socioeconomic data using a subsample of 1,380 abusive parents; the results suggested quite clearly that child abuse is more likely among lower-class parents: over 48% of the abusers had an annual income of under $5,000, while the percentage of all U. S. families at this income level is only 25.3. In addition, Gil reported that the abusive adults tend to be poorly educated: for mothers, less than 1% were college graduates, 4.4% had some college, and 17% were high school graduates. The majority had not completed high school (41%), and 24% had less than 9 years of schooling. A similar picture is present for fathers, with 32% not completing high school and another 24% having had less than 9 years of formal education. In light of the careful, comprehensive nature of the Gil survey, should we conclude that child abuse is more prevalent at lower socioeconomic levels? It is probably premature to draw this conclusion, since there are many reasons which make it difficult to secure reliable estimates of the incidence of child abuse across social classes. First, middle-class families are less likely to use the services of public agencies, clinics, and hospitals in the event of abuse; rather, they are able to afford the services of a private physician, who, in turn, may fail to report the incident in order to protect the family's privacy. Consideration of the Gil survey in view of this possibility casts some doubt on the extent to which all social class groups are represented in the survey results. The official sources reporting the incidents were principally hospitals (49%), police (23%), and public social agencies (8%). Private physicians and private social agencies reported only 2.9% of the cases. The importance of these figures stems from the fact that these private sources are more likely to be utilized by middle- and upper-class abusing adults. In short, lower-class abusers may be overrepresented in the Gil data. There are other reasons that preclude any strong conclusions about social class and child abuse. The living conditions (i.e., single-family dwellings) of middle-class parents may decrease the likelihood of detection by neighbors and others in the community. Third, community agencies may be less likely to intervene in middle- and upper-class homes (Solomon 1973). Fourth, some writers (Elmer 1967; Paulson & Blake 1969; Young 1964) note that higher socioeconomic class parents may be more deceptive and suspicious and make greater effort to conceal their abusive behavior.

Another set of data which casts doubt on a class-linked model of abuse comes from Gil's (1970) national survey of opinion and attitudes toward abuse. Gil inquired how his respondents thought they would react upon learning of an incident of abuse in their neighborhood. Only 7% would not involve themselves, and there were few social class differences. There is no evidence to support the view that lower-class adults are indifferent to the occurrence of abuse or are more likely to condone abuse than adults from higher social classes. At present, no clear-cut conclusions concerning the incidence of abuse across social class can be drawn. However, it is clear that some abuse does occur at all social class levels.

The particular source of stress that may elicit abuse, on the other hand, may be class-related. To date most of the literature has focused on those sources of stress that are more likely to affect lower-class families, such as unemployment, poor housing, and limited income. While we will examine these factors as possible contributors of abuse, it should be noted that the general stress model of abuse is not limited to the lower social class; middle-class families may encounter a variety of stresses which, in turn, may contribute to abuse. Job-elicited tension, marital disputes, and disobedient children are not limited to a single class; and more attention could profitably be paid to these sources of stress that are common to families at all social class levels.

3. Housing and Living Conditions

Is there a relationship between the type of housing and the type of parental disciplinary tactics generally and child abuse specifically? Unfortunately, systematic evidence of the impact of different physical aspects of the environment on the choices of socializing tactics of adults is nearly totally absent. Although earlier studies of crowding in animals (Calhoun 1962) found clear relationships between crowding and aggression, caution must be exercised in generalizing these findings to humans (Lawrence 1974). Some recent studies (Loo 1972) report no increase in interpersonal aggression among children of nursery school age as the amount of physical play space decreases. On the other hand, recent studies with adults suggest that reducing physical space may, in fact, influence propensities to aggression, particularly in males (Freedman 1973).

More relevant to the housing-discipline relationship is a study by Roy (1950) who found a direct relationship between the permissiveness of child-rearing attitudes as a function of the number of rooms in the house: fathers were more likely to endorse the use of power-assertive disciplinary tactics as household space decreased. However, the effect held only for fathers: mothers' attitudes did not vary with the availability of space. Whether parents and other socializing agents actually employ different types of disciplinary techniques as a function of house size is still to be determined. Other data (Newson & Newson 1968) derived from a study of English mothers found that punishment of lower-class children was significantly more frequent in unimproved and more densely populated housing. Frequency of interaction between parent and child may be higher in congested living quarters, thereby increasing the probability of conflict. Mitchell (1971), in a well-controlled study of high-density housing in Hong Kong, found that there is more hostility among families who live on upper floors of high-rise apartment buildings than those who reside on lower floors. The assumption is that lower-floor dwellers can more easily escape their living conditions by their easier access to outside areas. Living conditions may contribute to abuse in a variety of ways other than through modifying child-training practices. (See the chapter on ecology and development by Paul Gump in this volume for other relationships between housing and parental and child behavior.)

Parent interaction with neighbors may be affected by architectural and other housing variables (Festinger, Schachter & Back 1950; Mitchell 1971). Mitchell found that high-density housing discourages interaction and friendship practices among neighbors and friends; the higher the density, the less likely a family is to interact—even after family income is controlled. Social isolation—a factor that has been implicated in abuse (Young 1964)—may, in part, be determined by housing conditions.

There is little evidence that directly links housing and abuse; however, as we will note below, housing conditions may interact with other factors such as unemployment to jointly determine child abuse. But, first, unemployment as a contributor to abuse will be discussed.

4. Unemployment

A number of investigators have reported that unemployment may contribute to child abuse. Gil (1970) reported that only 52.5% of the fathers in his sample were employed throughout the year preceding the abuse incident. Twenty-seven percent of the fathers were unemployed part of the time, while 5.3% were unemployed for the whole year. In the case of working mothers, only 30.1% were consistently employed. Perhaps most important is the fact that nearly 12% of the fathers were actually unemployed at the time of the abuse incident, which, as Gil points out, is three times as high as the national unemployment rate. These unemployment figures were even higher for nonwhite fathers. Galdston (1965) and Young (1964) report similar findings in support of the unemployment–child abuse relationship.

Nor is it limited to child abuse; rather, unemployment appears to be related to other forms of intrafamily violence as well. Steinmetz and Straus (1974) note that there was a sharp rise in wife beating in England during a 6-month period when unemployment rapidly increased. More generally, this suggests that it is not just unemployment per se, but unexpected and sudden unemployment that would be most likely to elicit violent behavior. Support for this proposition derives from recent applications of expectancy theory to analyses of violence among the poor (Baron 1970; Berkowitz 1972; Gurin & Gurin 1970). There are a number of reasons for these relationships. First, a father who is unemployed is available in the home a larger portion of time, thereby increasing the probability of conflict arising either between husband and wife or father and children. Second, if available, the father may assume a greater role as disciplinarian than before. Third, some theorists (O'Brien 1971) have interpreted the unemployment–child abuse relationship in terms of status loss for the father. Viewing status as deriving from occupational achievement, failure to maintain job status may lead to attempts to assert greater authority in the family as a way of re-establishing his status and self-esteem. "Violent behavior was found to be most common in families where the husband was not achieving well in the work earner role and where the husband demonstrated certain status characteristics lower than those of his wife. This was viewed as a special form of status inconsistency. . . . Violent behavior represented the use of coercive, physical force by the husband in an effort to re-affirm his superior ascribed sex-role status vis-à-vis the other family members" (O'Brien 1971, p. 698). Fourth, unemployment may be associated with other frustrating circumstances such as lack of monetary resources. Steinmetz and Straus (1974) argue that unemployment may not directly affect the female, since her status is less likely to be job-defined; however, the reduced resources associated with unemployment that make her role as homemaker more difficult to fulfill adequately may be a source of dissatisfaction.

These relationships between intrafamily aggression and unemployment are consistent with other findings concerning job satisfaction. Gil (1974) has argued that the serious work alienation experienced by large segments of the working force may be a contributor to child abuse and other forms of familial violence. Some indirect evidence in support of Gil's position derives from McKinley's (1964) finding that the lower the job satisfaction, the higher the percentage of fathers who employed harsh punishment with their children—a relationship that held across social class levels. In summary, both unemployment and general job dissatisfaction are significant factors in child abuse.

In the next section, the relationships between the structure and organization of the family and child abuse will be examined.

5. *Family Size and Ordinal Position*

Another factor that is related to child abuse is family size. This would be expected on the assumption that an above-average number of children would be stressful for a caretaker. A number of investigators have found this relationship.

Gil (1970) has found that the proportion of families with three or more children is higher among families of child abuse than among the total U.S. population. In fact, the proportion of families with four or more children was nearly twice as high for his sample as for all families in the U.S. population. He also found that the proportion of larger families among nonwhite families in his sample was significantly higher than among white families.

Young (1964), in a rather broad-based sample of 180 families of abuse and neglect, found that only 20% of these had fewer than three children, and 37% had between six and 12 children. Johnson and Morse (1968), in their study of 101 children in Denver, found that two-thirds of the families had three or fewer children; 33% had four or more children; 2% had eight or more. Although these figures are certainly less extreme than Young's, they still indicate larger families among abusive families than families in the United States as a whole. Elmer (1967), looking at 20 abusive families, four nonabusive families, and seven unclassified (possible abuse?) families, found that the abusive families had a greater average number of children than the other groups and than the general population.

Light (1973) has offered the most extensive analysis of this problem in a comparison of the family size of child abusers in three countries: United States, New Zealand, and England. As table 1 illustrates, in all three countries approximately one-third of families who have children under 18 years of age have only a single child. However, the percentage of one child abusing families is much lower: 18% in the United States, 13.5% in New Zealand, and 23% in England. On the other end of the scale, 39.5% of U.S. abusing families have four or more children, which is twice as

TABLE 1

FAMILY SIZE AND BIRTH ORDER IN THREE COUNTRIES

	U.S.A.	
Number of Children	Abusing Families; Percentage in Gil Survey	U.S. Census Family Size Distribution Families with Children under 18
1................	18.0	31.8
2................	22.3	29.7
3................	20.2	18.9
4 or more........	39.5	19.6
	100.0	100.0
	New Zealand	
Number of Children	Abusing Families; Percentage in DSW Survey	New Zealand Family Size Distribution Families with Children under 18
1................	13.5	33.2
2................	19.2	30.8
3................	20.8	21.9
4 or more........	46.5	14.1
	100.0	100.0
	England	
Number of Children	Abusing Families; Percentage in NSPCC Survey	England Family Size Distribution Families with Children under 18
1................	23.1	34.4
2................	44.8	33.2
3................	19.2	20.5
4 or more........	12.9	11.9
	100.0	100.0

SOURCE.—Richard Light, "Abuse and Neglected Children in America: A Study of Alternative Policies," *Harvard Educational Review* 43 (November 1973): 574. Copyright © 1973 by President and Fellows of Harvard College.

high (19.6%) as the national average for all U.S. families. Similarly, in New Zealand, 46.5% of the abusing families have a large family of four or more children in contrast to a national average in New Zealand of 14.1%.

In summary, family size appears to be a contributor to child abuse; alternatively, it is possible that parents who are unable to judge adequately the number of children they can properly care for may, in addition, be potentially abusive as well.

While a number of different investigators have noted that the child's ordinal position in the family hierarchy may play a role in abuse, few clear-cut conclusions are possible (Brett 1967; Cameron, Johnson, & Camps 1966; Tuteur & Glotzer 1966). Part of the difficulty in evaluating the conflicting evidence is the failure of the majority of studies to control for family size, a clear correlate of abuse.

6. *Family-Community Relationships: Social Isolation as a Factor in Child Abuse*

To the extent that abuse is the outcome of a mounting set of stresses, the availability of structural arrangements that can provide support in times of stress and/or some periodic alleviation of or sharing of responsibility for children may be an important determinant. In modern society, there has been a general trend in family structure from the extended family to a self-contained, nuclear family living arrangement. In addition there have been trends toward greater mobility, social isolation, and anonymity. Whether abusive parents are products of these general trends is unclear; however, there are considerable data which suggest that abusive parents are socially isolated with few personal or community-based relationships. Young (1964) found that 95% of her severe-abuse families and 83% of her moderate-abuse families had "no continuing relationships with others outside the family." Friendships that did develop usually ended after a few weeks or months in a violent quarrel and ensuing bitterness. Moreover, 85% of her abusive families showed no membership or participation in an organized group. Merrill (1962), too, found that 50% of his abusive families had no formal group association, and 28% had only one group association, which was most frequently the church. Elmer (1967) found a difference between abusive and nonabusive mothers on her anomie scale—a scale that measured distrust of society, retreat from society, and resulting isolation. In support of the self-imposed isolation view, Lenoski (1974), in a large and careful study, found that 89% of abusive parents who had telephones had unlisted numbers; in contrast, only 12% of the nonabusive parents had unlisted telephone numbers. In addition, this investigator found that 81% of his abuse families preferred to resolve crises alone in contrast to 43% of the nonabuse parents. However, other evidence suggests that this isolation may not be completely voluntary. Merrill (1962) reported that abuse families are not fully accepted by their communities: 36% were accepted only moderately well and 47% only minimally, while Schloesser (1964) found that a number of her families were actually rebuffed by the community.

Several other investigators have found a high mobility among these families (Gil 1970; Schloesser 1964), with the result being the same—few nearby relatives or other roots in the community. The special point of mobility is the consequent disappearance of the extended family, a social group that in the past provided a built-in protection in the immediate environment. The contemporary nuclear family is often adrift from its original community, and the loss of the extended family probably plays a role in psychosocial isolation. Elmer (1967) has also mentioned the extended family, more common among Negro mothers than white, as a possible reason why the birth of a premature child seems less stressful to Negro than white mothers. However, it is more than merely the presence of relatives. The type of contact between white and black mothers and their relatives also differs: instrumental support in the form of babysitting and housecleaning was more characteristic among black than white mothers (Giovannoni & Billingsley 1970). Finally, it should be noted that the extended family is just one more contextual support missing from abusive parents' lives. As Bakan (1971) points out: "Although certain natural forces may be conducive to making parents care for their children, nonetheless there must be adequate contextual supports for the parents in this enterprise. In the relative absence of social support, one may expect that contrary impulses arise, even if they are not always acted out" (1971, pp. 89–90).

Abusive parents not only isolate themselves from the community, but abusive parents, according to Young (1964) are more likely than neglectful parents to prevent the child from developing relationships or friendships with other individuals outside the home and immediate family. The kind of community isolation that characterized the parents' own social behavior is apparently imposed on their children as well. Second, abusive families consistently denied normally accepted activities to children; the parents refused to allow children to participate in the usual recreational and educational opportunities, such as organized sports, parties, and informal neigborhood activities. The development of ordinary childhood friendships with peers is impossible under these circumstances. The family pattern of isolation has both immediate and long-range implications. To the extent that a cumulative stress model of abuse is appropriate, whereby a parent may become increasingly upset by a continuing number of minor misbehaviors, any set of factors that maintain the child in the immediate presence of the parent is likely to increase the possibility of abuse. Since childhood friendships often provide the basis for future adult friendships, the fact that the child is prevented from developing a network of friends merely increases the family isolation. Since social skills, including empathetic capacities, are learned through interactions with peers, the child's social development may be curtailed (Hartup 1970). Observations of the peer interactions of young abused children (under 4 years of age) in a nursery school setting confirms this expectation (Galdston 1971). There is little social interaction among the children, except unpredictable aggression among the boys. Galdston describes the abused children as "listless, apathetic, and uninterested in other children, toys or adults" (1971, p. 339).

Finally, preventing the child from forming friends makes it more likely that the child will continue a similar pattern of isolation as an adult. In summary, social isolation of both parent and child is characteristic of abusive families; again, the direction of causality is not clear. Possibly, abusive parents isolate themselves to avoid detection; on the other hand, abusive parents may lack the social skills that are necessary to form and maintain friendships and community ties. There is a third alternative, namely, that others may avoid abusive and potentially abusive parents because acquaintances may disapprove of the way in which these parents treat their children.

7. Toward Multiple-Cause Prediction of Abuse

In prior sections, the sociological variables that may contribute to abuse have been considered separately. However, it is unlikely that any single factor, *alone*, will be successful in accounting for abuse. Two recent investigators have moved to multiple-factor models of abuse.

First, Light (1973) has reported a statistically sophisticated re-analysis of Gil's original findings, using a multidimensional contingency table analysis which permits a preliminary isolation of two-variable relationships that discriminate abusing from nonabusing families. Light's analysis is a significant advance, since it introduces appropriate comparisons with nonabusing families. Much of the descriptive material in the child abuse literature is difficult to evaluate because such comparison rates in the nonabusing population are absent. A number of preliminary, but suggestive, findings emerged from the Light re-analysis. First, the unemployment status of the father was a discriminating variable but interacted with housing variables: "Abusing families where the father is unemployed are much more likely to live in an apartment than in a house relative to comparable non-abusing families where the father is unemployed. . . . Second, abusing families with an unemployed father/or a less educated father are much less likely to 'share their quarters' with other persons or families" (Light 1973, p. 587). Abusing families where the father is unemployed tend to have more children. Similarly, abusing families with less educated mothers or fathers tend to have more children. Finally, among abusing families, the father's unemployment status is related to the type of target; if the father is unemployed, abuse is more likely to be directed against a very young child. If the father is employed, abuse is more likely to be directed against an older child. Father's employment is the variable that shows up most often in the Light re-analysis and is consistent with a sociological emphasis on family stress due to unemployment.

Another multifactor approach to child abuse has recently been reported by Garbarino (1975). One of the problems that plague research on child abuse is the inconsistency in reporting across counties, cities, and states. In 1964, New York State established a reporting law which requires reporting of incidents or suspected incidents of child abuse to county social service agencies; in turn, county rates of abuse are collected in a Central Registry Office. Garbarino, as a test of a sociological view of child abuse, examined variations in rates of child abuse as a function of a number of socioeconomic and demographic variables across 58 counties in New York State. U.S. Census data were used to characterize the socioeconomic status of the counties in the sample in order to evaluate the contribution of (1) family mobility or transcience, (2) general economic development, (3) educational level, (4) rural-urban differences, and (5) the socioeconomic situation of mothers in the county. In addition, the rates of child abuse in each county were available.

This data base permitted a test of the hypothesis that the socioeconomic support system for the family in each county is directly associated with the rate of child abuse/maltreatment for that county: where support systems are better, where the family has more human resources, the rate of child abuse/maltreatment will be lower, and vice versa (Garbarino 1975, p. 9). First, use of a standard correlational approach, in which the separate contribution of each economic factor to child abuse was considered, yielded only a few significant relationships. The percentage of women with children under 18 in the labor force was positively related to abuse($r = .42$), while the median income of families headed by a female and the median income of all families were both negatively related to child abuse ($r = -.40$ and $-.27$, respectively). However, by the use of a multiple-regression approach, which controls for the intercorrelation among the socioeconomic and demographic indices, Garbarino was able to account for an impressive portion of the variance in child abuse across counties. Table 2 presents the results of this analysis, which suggests that five indices accounted for 36% of the total variance. This study provides impressive support for a sociological social stress analysis of child abuse; again, however, it should be noted that the child abuse incidence data were derived from public agency sources which overrepresent lower socioeconomic classes. Nevertheless, this study does suggest that environmental stress induced by variations in the availibility of socioeconomic resources—even within lower-class groups—is related to child abuse.

TABLE 2

Multiple Regression of Correlates of Child Abuse (Rate per 10,000 Population)

(1) Percentage of women in the labor force who have children under 18 years of age...	$r = .42$
(1) + (2) Median income of households headed by females............	$r = .47$
(1) + (2) + (3) Percentage of 3–4-year-olds enrolled in schools........	$r = .55$
(1) + (2) + (3) + (4) Percentage of 18–19-year-olds enrolled in schools	$r = .58$
(1) + (2) + (3) + (4) + (5) Percentage who are high school graduates..	$r = .60$

Source:—Garbarino 1975.

While neither of these studies can be viewed as definitive without replication, the multiplicative model of abuse underlying these investigations should be adopted in future studies. While single variables may be easier for conceptual and empirical analysis, only by moving beyond single-variable approaches will significant progress be made in understanding child abuse—a clearly multidetermined phenomenon.

8. Summary

In this section the sociological approach to child abuse which emphasizes the social-cultural context of abuse was presented. The prevailing condoning attitude toward violence in the American culture is assumed to be a determinant of abuse. Of particular importance for an understanding of child abuse is the widespread acceptance of physical punishment as a child-rearing technique. While abuse rates do vary across cultures, it is difficult to accurately assess the extent of abuse across social classes within our own culture. A variety of stress factors, such as unemployment and poor housing, were found to correlate with abuse rates. More attention should be paid to the types of stress in middle-class families that may elicit child abuse. The relationships between structure and organization of the family and child abuse were examined. Both family size and the child's ordinal position may be related to child abuse. While abuse rates are lower in small families, the current data on ordinal position of the child permit no firm conclusion. The isolation from the rest of the community is another characteristic of abusive families. Finally, it was argued that multiple-factor models of abuse are necessary, and some illustrative data in support of this approach were offered.

C. SOCIAL-SITUATIONAL MODEL OF CHILD ABUSE

Social-situational factors may contribute in a variety of ways to child abuse. First, the social situation in which the child is reared may determine the extent to which he himself is abusive as an adult. Second, the type of interaction patterns between child and adult or husband and wife may yield clues concerning the conditions under which potentially abusive patterns develop and the specific stimuli which serve to trigger or elicit abusive behavior. Third, a social-situational analysis may yield clues concerning the factors which may maintain abusive patterns. Let us examine each of these facets of a social-situational analysis.

1. The Eliciting and Accelerating Phases of Abuse

The effects of punitive child rearing.—A number of studies have documented the observation that abusive parents were themselves abused as children. This is a special manifestation of a more general relationship which suggests that the use of physical punishment by parents is associated with high aggression outside the home as children and as adults (Erlanger 1974). Probably these patterns are learned through imitation, and there is now a large body of research documenting the effects of exposure to aggressive models on the subsequent aggressive behavior of observers (see Stein & Freidrich, this volume). Translated into the disciplinary context, Bandura (1967) expressed this relationship as follows: "When a parent punishes his child physically for having aggressed toward peers, for example, the intended outcome of this training is that the child should refrain from hitting others. The child, however, is also learning from parental demonstration how to aggress physically. And the imitative learning may provide the direction for the child's behavior when he is similarly frustrated in subsequent social interactions" (1967, p. 43).

Similarly, adult physically punitive disciplinary patterns are probably shaped by early exposure to these patterns in childhood. Consistent exposure to these patterns may serve to sanction these types of behavior so that the adults view physical discipline as normative behavior for child rearing. Second, inhibitions against the use of physical force generally are lessened as a result of the legitimacy of physical punishment in child rearing.

This early establishment of physically punitive tactics as legitimate techniques for the solution of conflict may, in part, aid in understanding the relationship between physical punishment and child abuse. To the extent that physical punishment is used as a control tactic, this general class of physically violent responses, such as hitting, will be well rehearsed and high in the repertoire of available responses. A number of studies (e.g., Davitz 1952) have shown that, under conditions of stress and frustration, predominant responses are likely to be emitted; in short, the typical use of physically punitive responses in disciplinary contexts makes it more likely that these same types of responses will be employed in anger-eliciting situations. This assumes, of course, that some abuse occurs under circumstances where adults may react impulsively and involuntarily and cause injury that was not fully anticipated. Just as in murder, abuse is not necessarily rational and deliberate. As Berkowitz recently argued: "Most homocides are 'spontaneous acts of passion' arising from fights over trivial issues. Relatively few are the product of thought-out determination to kill (Mulvihill and Tumin, 1969; Wolfgang, 1968). These violent outbursts are often too impulsive, too quick and involuntary to be greatly affected by the aggressor's belief as to what will be the outcome of their behavior, beyond the simple idea they will hurt their victim. . . . In their rage they strike out without much thought" (1974, p. 165). At least some child abuse may begin in a similar, nondeliberate fashion, and it is assumed that the ready availability of aggressive responses used in a disciplinary context makes abuse more likely.

There are other reasons for the physical punishment–child abuse relationship. There is an interesting discrepancy between attitude and usage in the realm of physical punishment. Many who use physically punitive tactics tend to disapprove of these techniques. In contrast, in the past, there was less discrepancy between attitudes and usage. As a result of this cultural shift in attitude, the manner in which physical punishment is employed makes the contemporary use of this type of discipline potentially more dangerous than in the past. When punishment was viewed as an appropriate and justifiable tactic, it was used in a more measured and deliberate fashion. As a disciplinary technique, punishment was delivered not necessarily in anger but under controlled circumstances in which both victim and punishing agent were aware of the reason for the action and the limits of the dosage. Not only was punishment likely to be more effective in achieving control, due to the clear understanding concerning the relationship between the disapproved act and the punishment, but under these controlled circumstances of delivery, escalation— as might occur under conditions of anger—would be less likely to occur. Physical punishment in contemporary child rearing, especially in middle-class homes, is more typically an impulsive, angry reaction than a deliberate, disciplinary action. This discrepancy in terms of norms and actual usage may be creating the potential for abuse.

Inconsistent use of discipline.—Another reason for the possible link between physical punishment and child abuse is the inconsistent fashion in which physical punishment is employed by abusive parents. A pattern of inconsistent discipline is typical of abusing parents. Young (1964) reported that virtually all of the abusing families were inconsistent in disciplining their children (100% of the severe-abuse and 91% of the moderate-abuse families). Similarly, 88% of the severe-abuse and 81% of the moderate-abuse families showed "no consistent expectations" for their children; in less than one-quarter of the abusive families were the children given any defined responsibilities. These findings indicate a total absence of guidelines or consistent discipline in the abusive families. Discipline is consistent instruction and must conform with some established rules or standards; these standards must have continuity. In contrast, parental punishment of children in the abused families was divorced from the specific behavior of the children; it became, in effect, punishment for its own sake. "The severity and brutality of parental abuse and its lack of corrective purpose distinguish it clearly from the customary concept of punishment of children" (Young 1964, p. 181). Moreover, the reasons which these parents gave for their behavior were typically inappropriate and illogical, nor did they recognize any discrepancy between the intensity of the punishment and the minor seriousness of the child's misbehavior.

An examination of the marital roles of the parents reveals further inconsistency. Young found that "parents have defined responsibilities" in only 33% of the severe-abuse and 21% of the moderate-abuse families. Each of the following categories held true for about 60% of the severe group: "one parent imposes controls," "one parent plans use of money," "one parent makes all or most decisions," However, in 88% of the families "neither parent takes responsibility for decisions," which indicates a marked separation of authority and responsibility in the abuse families; the parent making the decisions shifts the responsibility for them; the result is poor child control and a low level of predictability for the child. Neither parent nor child can depend on any consistent interaction pattern.

Elmer (1967) reported similar findings in her comparison of abusive and nonabusive families. In terms of household organization, the abusive mothers were low in comparison to the nonabusive mothers. In terms of discipline, she found that the nonabusive families tended to use a few types of discipline consistently; in contrast, the abusive families used a broad range of tactics in an inconsistent manner.

What are the effects of inconsistent discipline? Data from field studies of delinquency have yielded a few clues concerning the consequences of inconsistency of discipline. Glueck and Glueck (1950) found that parents of delinquent boys were more "erratic" in their disciplinary practices than were parents of nondelinquent boys. Similarly, the McCords (e.g., McCord, McCord, & Howard 1961) have found that erratic disciplinary procedures were correlated with high degrees of criminality. Inconsistent patterns involving a combination of love, laxity, and punitiveness, or a mixture of punitiveness and laxity alone, were particularly likely to be found in the background of their delinquent sample.

Laboratory studies of the effects of inconsistent punishment on children's aggression have indicated that intermittent punishment administered by a single agent is a less effective technique than consistent punishment for controlling aggressive behavior (Parke & Deur 1972). Nor is it simply intraagent inconsistency that produces poor control; as Stouwie (1972) has demonstrated, inconsistency between two socializing agents also leads to ineffective control of children's behavior.

Other investigations indicate that inconsistent discipline has long-term implications for the control of child behavior. Parents and other socializing agents often use consistent punishment after inconsistent punishment has failed to change the child's behavior. To investigate the effectiveness of consistent punishment after the child has been treated in an inconsistent fashion was the aim of another study by Deur and Parke (1970). Specifically, these investigators found that children who are inconsistently disciplined by occasionally being rewarded and at other times punished for aggressive behavior persisted in their aggressive behavior for a longer period—under conditions of either extinction or consistent punishment—than boys who had not previously experienced the inconsistent treatment. The implication is clear: the socializing agent using inconsistent punishment builds up resistance to future attempts to either extinguish deviant behavior or suppress it by consistently administered punishment.

The acceleration of low-intensity punishment to high-intensity levels.— There is another outcome of the inconsistent use of punishment that may aid in understanding the punishment-abuse relationship, namely, the acceleration of low-intensity punitive responses into more intense and therefore potentially abusive responses. This acceleration process is, in fact, one of the central problems that must be faced by a social-situational analysis. In other words, how are high-intensity responses shaped up so that they are available for elicitation under stressful conditions? The erratic use of punishment and the resulting weak control of behavior may be one factor in accounting for acceleration. As the child's behavior persists in the face of inconsistent handling, the parents, in order to control the child's behavior, may accelerate the intensity of their punitive tactics. Since other research (Parke 1969) indicates that high-intensity punishment is more effective than low-intensity punishment, the socializing agent may, in fact, be reinforced for their use of high-intensity tactics. However, if the punishment is erratic, only momentary control will be achieved and the parent may, in turn, resort to a more intense punishment on some future occasion. It is quite possible that abusive levels of punishment could develop out of this type of parent-child interaction in a disciplinary context.

Patterson has conceptualized a related type of interaction pattern in which there is acceleration of aversive stimuli exchanged by participants as the coercion process (Patterson & Cobb 1971, 1973; Patterson & Reid 1970). According to this view, when one person presents an aversive stimulus, the second person is likely to respond with an aversive stimulus if the initial aversive stimulus appears alterable. The aversive interchange continues and escalates in intensity until one person withdraws his aversive stimulus; at this point, the other person would withdraw his aversive stimulus. The coercion paradigm provides a fruitful framework for elucidating the contribution of the child's behavior to the development of parental abuse patterns. The coercion paradigm describes how the intensity of parental disciplinary responses could be escalated in response to aversive stimuli presented by the child until physical abuse results. Studies (Patterson & Cobb 1971) in the home context illustrate this process. In detailed observations of the interaction patterns among family members, they found that aversive stimuli such as commands or teasing accelerated the probablity that the target child would hit; similarly, hitting increased hitting in the victim. In a related study (Patterson & Cobb 1973), they isolated the clusters of stimuli that elicited either social aggression (physically aggressive behavior or teasing) or hostility (negativism, disapproval, humiliation, whining). A specific example will illustrate the nature of this stimulus control. The baseline probability of hit was .003, but if a younger sister teased the target child, the probability increased to .067. In turn, if the subject hit the sister and she returned the hit, the probability of another hit was .44. These examples illustrate the manner in which the intensity of responses can be accelerated in dyadic interaction contexts.

Although Patterson's work has implicated peers and siblings as shapers of aggression, these high-intensity aggressive responses on the part of children may, in turn, elicit high-intensity disciplinary tactics from parents in order to suppress these behaviors. It is hypothesized that the success that a parent may have in inhibiting highly disruptive behaviors through the use of high-intensity tactics serves to maintain these tactics. Patterson and Cobb spell out the possible implications of their model for abuse as follows:

In the case of mothers, it is hypothesized that there are many grown women with no past history of Hitting, who are shaped by interactions with infants and children to initiate physical assaults. Presumably the shaping process is analogous to that provided by children, for children. The mother learns that Hits terminate aversive child behavior. She may then be trained to display behavior of increasingly high amplitude as a function of contingencies supplied by children. We also suspect that many of the child homicides reported are in fact the outcome of such training programs. A young woman, unskilled in mothering, is trained by her own children to carry out assaults that result in bodily injury to her trainers. [Patterson & Cobb 1971, p. 124]

In fact, Reid (1974, personal communication) has indicated that approximately one-quarter of the parents of the aggressive boys in these studies would be classified as abusive. In a later section, ways of modifying parent and child behaviors that are maintained by this coercion process will be examined.

An illustration of the combined operation of both coercion and inconsistent discipline in the development of tantrum behavior in an 8-year-old child is provided by Bernal et al. (1968). They noted that the child is able to force maternal compliance by verbal and physical threats; in turn, the mother's acquiescence in the face of the threats increased the probability of further threatening and tantrum behavior. Control attempts typically took the form of an occasional severe spanking, but these spankings were inconsistently delivered and provided little unambiguous information concerning the nature of inappropriate behavior. In addition, threats to punish were seldom accompanied by follow-up punishment. As noted above, inconsistent punishment is ineffective in controlling behavior. This erratic use of punishment and the exercises in hollow threatening combined with submission in the face of high-magnitude noncompliant tactics served to accelerate the child's behavior; in turn, to control these behaviors, the parent may accelerate the punitive tactics in attempting to inhibit the behavior. In combination, the concepts of inconsistent discipline and coercion suggest a reasonable framework within which the acceleration of parental punishment to abusive levels can be understood.

Generalization.—Why is the child often a victim of intrafamily violence? While abuse may be directly triggered by children's behavior, abuse, on other occasions, may be the outcome of husband-wife violence. Particularly in cases where there are strong norms limiting this type of conflict, the child may become a victim. Alternatively, aggression may be directed toward the child when extreme dominant-submissive patterns between the parents prevent a passive parent from directly expressing aggression toward the spouse. In fact, Terr (1970) has reported exaggerated dominant-submissive patterns in abusive families. Fenigstein and Buss (1974) recently provided evidence in support of the concept of selective aggression against a weak victim. Adults were angered and then given the opportunity to deliver a mildly noxious stimulus to a confederate who was associated with the insulting experimenter or aggress in a more intense manner against a nonassociated individual. The angered subjects preferred the target that allowed the display of the most intense aggression rather than the victim most similar to the original anger inducer. A similar process may operate in family contexts.

2. Maintaining Conditions for Abuse

Another question that requires attention are the conditions that maintain repeated abuse. There are many reasons for the finding that patterns of abuse are maintained. One aspect of this maintenance issue is post-abuse justification. In light of apparent harm, adults may engage in a series of tactics designed to minimize, justify, or shift responsibility for the abuse. An understanding of these processes may also aid in understanding the low reporting rate among abusing parents.

Justification of abuse.—A common tactic is justification of abuse in terms of higher principles. The abuse is viewed as part of necessary and morally justified discipline, the intent of the discipline being to establish appropriate social and moral conduct (Steele & Pollock 1968). In such cases, cooperation with authorities is often low; authorities are viewed as interfering with parental rights to choose their own methods of discipline and child care. In such cases, guilt and remorse which, in turn, may serve to inhibit later abusive attacks (Berkowitz 1962) are lacking, which, in turn, will increase the probability of future abuse.

Minimization of abuse.—Another factor which may maintain abuse is the minimization of the incident and the selective forgetting of the consequences (Bandura 1973). Individuals often execute acts of harmful abuse under conditions of anger in spite of the fact that these acts are inconsistent with their expressed values. Brock and Buss (1964) have shown that individuals who display aggressive acts of which they disapprove tend to selectively recall information concerning the potential benefits of such behavior while being less able to remember the harmful effects.

Shifting of responsibility.—There are other factors as well. The parent may blame the child for his behavior: "the child drove me to it," By shifting responsibility to the victim, there is a decreased likelihood of the abusive parent modifying his behavior. This shifting of responsibility may take other forms, such as displacing responsibility to another family member such as a spouse *or*, alternatively, not sharing responsibility with a spouse. Characteristic of severely abusive families is an unwillingness to take responsibility for decisions (Young 1964, p. 168).

Partner reactions to abuse.—Another factor that contributes to the maintenance of abuse is the reaction of a partner or spouse. Peer reaction can both maintain and inhibit aggressive behavior. In a situation in which adults were required to deliver increasingly harmful aggressive responses to a victim, the presence of two supportive peers increased the level of aggressiveness that the subject was willing to display. Alternatively, the presence of partners who refuse to escalate their level of aggressiveness served to lower the subject's aggressive behavior (Milgram 1974). In the abuse context, the reactions of a spouse or coobserver can clearly modify the extent of abuse and the probability of repeated occurrence. While abuse may, in part, be more likely in single-parent homes due to the lack of a partner who can intervene and prevent serious acceleration of punishment to damaging levels, no simple prediction is possible without exploration of the attitudes of the partner. However, it may be that abuse is often maintained due not to explicit approval by the partner but simply by the partner's indifference or nonreaction. Nonreaction in situations involving serious harm may, in fact, function as positive reinforcement or approval (Bandura 1965).

Derogation of victim.—Derogation of the victim is another device used to justify family violence. By attributing a sufficient number of negative characteristics to the victim, any dissonance associated with the abuse can be reduced. Young (1964) has reported that over 90% of the severely abusive families engaged in verbally abusive language such as name calling, insulting, and mockery. For example, "parents stated bluntly that they hated the children . . . others remarked they had never liked them. A parent referred frequently to his son as 'crazy,' 'the idiot' or a child was repeatedly told he was 'dumb.' In other cases a parent emphasized how physically ugly a child was or called him 'the criminal' " (Young 1964, p. 159). These reactions characterized 85% of the severe-abuse families, 55% of the moderately abusive families, and only 40% and 22% of the severe- and moderate-neglect families. It is easy to attack a victim whom you have despised and labeled in ways that make him undesirable.

There is another aspect that merits consideration. Not only do physically abusive parents derogate the child victim, but there is a high degree of verbal abuse and criticism. The high rate of verbal aggression may not only serve to justify physical violence but, in fact, may stimulate the parents to engage in physical violence. A number of experimental studies (Loew 1967; Parke, Ewall, & Slaby 1972) have demonstrated that speaking aggressively may stimulate and make more likely subsequent physically aggressive actions as well. Straus (1974) has recently found that there is a close positive relationship between verbal and physical violence in husband-wife conflicts.

Pain feedback.—Another factor that may play an important role in regulating the degree of abusive behavior is the pain feedback from the victim. Pain cues may function either to maintain an ongoing aggressive sequence or inhibit the attacker's aggression. In well-socialized adults, pain feedback from the victim will decrease the intensity of an aggressive attack (Baron 1971; Buss 1966). In fact, aggression is even more readily inhibited if the attacker is directly exposed to the visual and auditory signs of suffering. Although knowledge that a prior action caused another person to suffer can inhibit (Buss 1966), the pain cues that the victim displays during an aggressive encounter can also function to reduce the intensity of the attack (Baron 1971). Moreover, the inhibitory impact of pain feedback is most marked when the aggressor can directly witness the visual and auditory pain cues of the victim (Milgram 1974). In an abusive exchange between parent and child where the parent is directly exposed to the suffering of the child, why does the pain feedback not function as an inhibitor? There are a number of possible reasons. First, Feshbach and Feshbach (1969) have demonstrated that the inhibitory effect of pain feedback may be dependent on the development of empathy; research on abusive parents (Spinetta & Rigler 1972) suggests that abusive parents are relatively low in empathy and, therefore, may be unresponsive to the signs of suffering in their victims. In part, it may be due to the failure of the abusive parent to react with inhibition to low-intensity signs of suffering that permits the escalation of punitiveness to abusive extremes. In nonabusive parents, early and subtler signs of pain function to regulate and prevent extremely harmful forms of aggression from occurring. There is evidence which indicates that highly aggressive individuals, particularly if angered, may accelerate the intensity of their attacks in response to the sight of pain on the part of the victim. Hartmann (1969) exposed juvenile delinquent males to a film which graphically displayed the suffering of a victim of an aggressive attack. In contrast to those exposed to a film emphasizing the instrumental features of an aggressive encounter, the boys who watched the pain-cues film more vigorously attacked an opponent when they were angered. The delinquents with the longest records of prior offenses were most strongly affected by the pain cues. It appears that individuals who have well-established aggressive patterns of behavior may be particularly likely to react to a victim's suffering with strong attacks.

Summary.—In this section the social-situational model of child abuse was outlined. This approach stresses the ways in which abusive patterns may develop from the use of physically punitive discipline. It was demonstrated that the abusing parents' own history of physically punitive rearing predisposes them to employ similar tactics in controlling their own children. A variety of factors, including parental inconsistency in the execution of discipline, were examined to explain the possible manner in which low-intensity punitive responses are accelerated into more intense abusive behaviors. On occasion, the child may be the victim of the generalization of husband-wife violence. Next, a series of processes which account for the maintainance of child abuse were examined. Post-abuse justification in terms of higher principles, minimization of the harm, derogation of the victim, and shifting of responsibility were noted as tehniques that may account for the maintainance of abusive patterns. The role that the partner may play in the maintainance process was also discussed.

D. THE CHILD'S ROLE IN ABUSE

A serious shortcoming in both the psychiatric and sociological models is their failure to give adequate recognition to the interactive nature of child abuse. It is insufficient to view abuse from a unidirectional view-point, whereby the main cause is located in either the parent or in exter-nal social circumstances. One important feature of the social-situational approach is the recognition that both partners, the child victim as well as the parent, need to be considered if child abuse is to be fully understood. In particular, the role that the child himself may play in eliciting abuse needs to be more closely examined. With few exceptions (Milowe & Lowrie 1964; Sameroff & Chandler 1975), this issue has received little attention in the past. A number of clinical investigators have pointed to the *selectivity* of abuse; not all children are abused, but usually only a single child within a family is selected for the abusive treatment.

The child may contribute to his own abuse in a variety of ways. First, there may be some genetically determined physical and behavioral char-acteristics of the child that may make it more likely that he will be abused. Second, the child may develop behaviors through interaction with parents and peers that make him a likely target for abuse. Alterna-tively, as a result of physical abuse, the child may develop behavior patterns which, in turn, elicit more abuse from his caretakers or possibly from other caretakers, who themselves may not have originally maltreat-ed the child. Abuse, in other words, may shape up behavior patterns which increase the likelihood of further abuse. As Bakan (1971) notes, "the well taken care of child attracts positive responses. The child who is abused and neglected becomes ugly in appearance and behavior and invites further abuse and neglect" (p. 109). Of particular importance are the altered behavior patterns that may invite further abuse. While there are reports of the same child being abused in different foster homes (McKay, cited by Milowe & Lourie 1964), even professional personnel, such as nurses, find abused children difficult to manage and care for. A statement by Bain (cited by Bakan 1971) illustrates the reaction of nurses in one hospital setting: "We began discovering that the child in the bed farthest from the nurse's station was sometimes a child that fitted into this syndrome. . . . Somehow these children establish the same relationship to the nurses (as to their parents). When you walk through the ward you can judge by the number of toys on beds; these children have less toys. You can count the pictures in their rooms. Somehow the response they're getting from the nurse is less warm" (p. 110). It is clear that the child can contribute to his own abuse. Now let us examine the ways in which this may occur in more detail.

1. The Infant as a Target of Abuse

The birth of the newborn infant is often a stressful event which can affect the relationships among family members. There are many tasks that must be mastered, including not only routine caretaking but modifying schedules and activities to accomodate another individual. As Bakan (1971) notes: "the coming of the child tends to disturb the total equilibrium of the life of the parents, including the possibility of the child's creating disturbances in the sexual sphere, the social sphere, the occupational sphere and the total income of the parent. . . . Children constitute a burden calling for sacrifices on the part of the adult" (Bakan 1971, p. 90). Ryder (1973), in a unique longitudinal assessment of the impact that a new infant has on family relationships, confirmed this conclusion. Women who had a child, compared with those who did not, were less satisfied with their marriage and specifically reported that their husbands were not paying sufficient attention to them. The problem of adjusting to a newborn infant is exaggerated under a number of circumstances which may make abusive reactions more likely. For example, these dissatisfactions are probably exaggerated in the case of a child who is the product of an unwanted pregnancy—"a pregnancy which began before marriage, too soon after marriage, or at some time felt to be extremely inconvenient" (Kempe et al. 1962) and a number of studies (Birrell & Birrell 1968; Nurse 1964) have documented this conclusion. Moreover, as noted earlier, the arrival of another child in an already large family may strain the resources of the family so greatly that the new infant is abused.

Bell's (1968) distinction between parental upper- and lower-limit-control behaviors may be useful for understanding how the infant's behavior may contribute to his abuse. Upper-limit-control behavior of the parent includes those responses which regulate and reduce behavior of the child which exceeds parental expectations and standards of intensity, frequency, and competence for the child's age. Conversely, lower-limit-control behavior is that which stimulates child behavior which is below parental standards. Bell predicts, for example, that the parent will exhibit upper-limit-control behavior in response to excessive and sustained crying by an infant or to impulsive and hyperactive behavior by a child, whereas lethargic and apathetic behavior should elicit lower-limit-control behavior. Viewed from this vantage point, successful socialization involves the maintenance of the child's behavior within the upper and lower boundaries acceptable to the parent.

Many characteristics of the child could affect the frequency and threshold of parental upper- and lower-limit-control behavior and thus influence the probability of the occurrence of the coercive process (Patterson & Cobb 1973) that we described earlier. For example, infants who exhibit excessive and sustained crying may present particularly frequent and strong aversive stimuli to the mother and thus elicit upper control behavior.

There are individual differences in irritability and soothability which may be congenitally based (Freedman & Freedman 1969; Wolff 1969); moreover, there are wide individual differences in the ways in which distress can be successfully inhibited (Birns, Blank , & Bridger 1966). Typically, crying decreases over the first year of life (Bell & Ainsworth 1972; Parmalee 1972), and successful control of infant crying is a prerequisite for successful maintenance of the parent-infant dyad. However, failure to inhibit crying effectively can lead to a breakdown in the parent-child relationship. Robson and Moss (1970) noted decreases in mother-infant attachment after the first month as a result of sustained irritability (crying, fussing). Similarly, Bell and Ainsworth (1972) reported relationships between failure to control infant crying effectively and maternal withdrawal in the latter part of the first year. The breakdown of the affectional relationship may be the first step toward a potentially abusive outcome. To the extent that a mother withdraws and interacts less with her infant, the less likely that she will be able to notice and respond to low-intensity precursors of crying. Responding to the early cues may avert the high-intensity aspects of the sequence, such as agitated crying (Bell 1974), which, in turn, is probably more difficult to inhibit than the lower levels of distress. Unfortunately, the full-blown crying may be reinforced by maternal attention involved in attempting to inhibit it (Etzel & Gewirtz 1967). The result is a situation wherein the infant is shaped up to use high-intensity cues to elicit a maternal response; the parent, in turn, may also resort to high-intensity behaviors to control this aversive behavior. Initially, the maternal behavior may produce little harm and be of low intensity; however, as the infant sustains the crying, the mother may escalate her responses. This escalation may continue until eventually the mother uses high-intensity and harmful tactics in a desperate attempt to terminate her infant's crying.

Another important factor is the clearness or readability of the cues which an infant provides his mother. If an infant presents weak or unclear signals about the internal or external stimuli controlling his behavior (Korner 1974), his mother may have difficulty in determining how to terminate his aversive stimuli effectively, and thus the probability of the coercive process occurring may be increased. With respect to parents, a mother who is unskilled at detecting an infant's signals may have great difficulty in soothing her infant. Similarly, a mother who lacks a wide, flexible range of effective caretaking and disciplinary techniques is likely to have increased chances of becoming involved in the coercion process, simply because she possesses few effective means of terminating her infant or child's undesirable behavior. Alernatively, "Too often mothers cannot or will not respond to their infants' cues, either for reasons of their own psychology and needs or because of convictions they hold as to what contributes 'good childcare.' Such factors within the mother can seriously impede the beginning mother-child interaction and result in a mismatch of the pair" (Korner 1974, p. 117). Still another attribute of the mother which may affect her upper-limit-control behavior is her expectations of the child. The mother who sets excessively high standards for her child or who tolerates only very low-intensity aversive stimuli may be more likely to escalate her behavior to abusive levels when the child presents her with aversive stimuli.

Another way in which mismatching can occur is in terms of the mother and infant preferred modes of interaction. Some babies resist such forms of physical contact as being embraced, hugged, and held tight (Schaffer & Emerson 1964). This apparently genetically based interaction style may cause serious disruptions for certain types of mothers who prefer cuddly infants. Possible mismatches between parental styles may conceivably be an early precursor of poor attachment formation and possible later abuse. As Steele and Pollock (1968) note in their discussion of abusive parents: "Some parents are disappointed when they have a placid child instead of a hoped-for more reactive, responsive baby. Other parents are equally distressed by having an active, somewhat aggressive baby who makes up his own mind about things when they had hoped for a very placid compliant infant" (1968, p. 129).

Current research aimed at isolating the ways in which parent-infant dyads adapt (Osofsky & Danzger 1974; Parke & O'Leary 1975) should prove fruitful in the early identification of potential breakdowns in the parent-infant dyad.

However, lower limit control behaviors, which may occur in response to a lethargic and unresponsive infant, or in an infant who fails to meet parental expectations of normal development, may also contribute to the development of abusive patterns.   For example, Robson & Moss (1970) found that an infant who was late in exhibiting smiling and eye-to-eye contact elicited violent reactions in the mother and was later found to have suffered relatively serious brain damage (cited by Bell 1974). In addition, abuse is more likely in the case of the passive or lethargic infant or one who is developmentally retarded in their expression of new behaviors, because these characteristics may interfere with the development of a positive parent-child relationship. To the extent that an affectional tie between a caretaker and infant may function as a deterrent to the expression of abusive behaviors the infant who exhibits lower-limit behaviors may be a more likely candidate for abuse. The low birth weight infant that we will discuss in the next section is an example of this type of infant.

2. The Low Birth Weight Infant: A Special Target for Abuse?

An infant who is particulary likely to be abused is the low birth weight infant. Low birth weight, of course can take a variety of forms: (*a*) infants born at term to mothers of small stature, (*b*) infants born at or near term but markedly underweight as a result of intrauterine malnutrition, or (*c*) infants born after a relatively short gestation period. A baby of low birth weight born to a small mother may be a result of genetic factors and have low morbidity rates (Douglas, cited by Caputo & Mandell 1970). As Caputo and Mandell note, however, it is important to consider birth weight in conjunction with other variables such as gestational age. An infant whose birth weight is well below the mean for his gestational age (small-for-dates babies) is presumed to show retarded fetal growth and demonstrate prenatal and postnatal characteristics different from those of low birth weight infants of low gestational age. Unfortunately, too little attention has been paid to distinctions among low birth weight infants in terms of their potential for abuse.

The most convincing evidence of the association between low birth weight and child abuse comes from a study by Klein and Stern (1971). Using hospital records between 1960 and 1969, these investigators retrieved all charts containing diagnoses of "battered child syndrome," which was defined as "frank unexplained skeletal trauma or severe bruising or both, or such neglect as to lead to severe medical illness or immediate threat to life" (1971, p. 15). Of the 51 cases retrieved, 39 cases, or 76%, had been full-term infants and 12, or 23.5%, had been low birth weight infants (less than 2,500 grams). This proportion of low birth weight infants is significantly higher than the normal rate for low birth weight of 7%–8%. However, since mothers of low socioeconomic status are more likely to have children of low birth weight, Klein and Stern reexamined the birth weight–abuse relationship while controlling for the rate of low birth weight infants among lower-class mothers. Even employing a revised rate of 10% as the incidence of low birth weight for low socioeconomic mothers, the abuse incidence of 23.5% was still significantly higher than the expected percentage.

Other investigators have reported similar relationships. Simons et al. (1966) found that 20% of the abused babies in their New York sample for whom birth records were available were under 5 ½ pounds at birth—a percentage which is approximately twice that of the city as a whole. Similarly, Fontana (1968) reported that over 50% of the 25 maltreated children in his sample were of low birth weight, while Elmer and Gregg (1967) found 30% of their sample were under 2,400 grams at birth.

Some reasons for the low birth weight–child abuse relationship.—There are many factors that may account for the greater susceptibility of the low birth infant to abuse. Two sets of issues will be discussed: (1) the characteristics of the low birth weight infants that may make the caretaking task more difficult and (2) the structural arrangements surrounding the birth of a low birth weight infant, particularly parent-infant separation.

Characteristics of low birth weight infants.—The survival rate of the low birth weight infant has increased greatly in recent years due to advances in medical care and technology (Caputo & Mandell 1970; Klaus & Fanaroff 1973). While these advances are laudable, many of these "new" survivors often have serious medical difficulties as well as a higher rate of short-term and long-term developmental problems than normal infants. In a comprehensive review of the consequences of low birth weight, Caputo and Mandell (1970) point out a number of outcomes that may make the low birth weight infant more susceptible to parental abuse. It should be noted that some of the outcomes may alter the parent-child relationship in the early postpartum months, while others may not affect the parent-child dyad until the child is beyond infancy. Of course, the disturbances in parent-child interaction may, in fact, be important contributors to disturbances in later years. First, we will examine some of the short-term effects of low birth weight.

There are clear cultural norms concerning appropriate size, weight, and appearance for newborn infants; the parents' responsiveness is, in part, determined by the extent to which the infant's physical characteristics conform to parental expectations. In fact, there are certain characteristics of the normal human infant's face, such as the concavity of the face and the height of the eyes, which are responded to discriminatively and positively by adults (Brooks & Hochberg 1960). The low birth weight premature infant violates many parental expectations; it is not merely a matter of timing, but possibly it is the smallness and underdeveloped appearance of the premature infant which contributes to his eventual abuse as a result of parental failure to develop strong attachment to this "unattractive" infant.

Low birth weight infants place greater demands on their parents than normal infants. For example, feeding disturbances are more common among low birth weight infants. Due to their low weight, these infants must be fed more often, and especially in the case of very low birth weight infants, special feeding techniques may be necessary (Klaus & Fanaroff 1973). In addition, premature infants may cry more and be more irritable (Elmer 1967). In part, these difficulties may stem from the fact that medical problems are often associated with prematurity and low birth weight. For example, Klein and Stern (1971) reported that nine of their 12 low birth weight infants had major neonatal problems (e.g., exchange transfusion, pneumonia, birth asphyxia). In contrast, only 15 out of the 39 normal birth weight infants had medical or developmental complications. In turn, these infants may make more demands on their parents and caretaking may be a more difficult task.

In addition, low birth weight infants may continue to disappoint their parents, since their developmental progress in motor, social, and cognitive spheres is often retarded during at least the first 2 years (Wright 1971). These infants may develop more slowly in terms of social behavior as indexed by the Vineland Social Maturity Scale (Moore 1966); others report that prematures make fewer vocalizations prior to 8 months of age (Lezine 1958). Due to the slower development of social responsiveness, the infant may elicit less positive attention from his caretakers and be viewed as less interesting. On the motor and cognitive side, premature infants tend to walk later and use sentences later than controls (Rabinowitz, Bibace, & Caplan 1961). Nor are the problems restricted to infancy. Caputo and Mandell (1970) have noted a variety of post infancy problems including hyperactivity and childhood accidents. Finally, language development, reading, arithmetic, and spelling are often poorer among low birth weight infants. Although research is badly needed to specify the exact characteristics of the low birth weight infant that elicit parental abuse, it is clear that the burden, stress, and disappointment associated with the birth and care of a low birth weight infant could increase the probability of abuse. The low birth weight–abuse relationship is even more plausible in light of the extremely high and unrealistic expectations that many abusive parents have for their children's developmental progress (Steele & Pollock 1968); the discrepancy between parental expectations and child behavior is particularly marked in the case of the low birth weight infant.

Early maternal-infant separation.—There is another factor that merits consideration in untangling the low birth weight–abuse relationship, namely, the prolonged separation between mother and premature infant in the early postpartum period. It is assumed that the early postpartum period is important for the development of parent-infant attachment. Second, it is assumed that according to the extent to which there is parent-infant attachment, the likelihood of abusive behavior being directed toward the infant would be reduced. Finally, it is assumed that a caretaker who has the opportunity to form an attachment with his infant will be more sensitive to the infant's needs and signals and, therefore, more likely to effectively control potentially abuse-eliciting behaviors, such as irritability and crying.

The recent human research is based on earlier studies with animals (Collias 1956; Hersher, Moore, & Richmond 1958) which demonstrated that mothers may reject their young if they were separated from their newborn infants immediately after birth. These human studies of the effect of separation of mother and infant in the early postpartum period indicate that the type and amount of social interaction between mothers and their newborns during the immediate postpartum period have significant effects on the mother's subsequent attitudes and behavior toward her infant.

Evidence for the influence of mothers' early contact with their premature infants and their later caretaking skills is reported by Leifer, Leiderman, and Barnett (1970). Mothers who were given an opportunity to care for their premature infants in the intensive-care nursery were found to be significantly more skillful in a subsequent feeding session observed during the fifth visit to the discharge nursery than were the mothers who had not been permitted interaction with infants during the infant's earlier stay in the intensive-care nursery. Other research (Seashore et al. 1973) indicates that early separation results in lowered self-confidence among primiparous mothers in their performance of instrumental tasks (diapering, feeding, bathing) as well as social tasks (calming baby, recognizing infant's needs, showing affection).

Opportunities for early contact affect maternal attachment behavior as well as maternal attitudes. Mothers who were permitted physical contact with their premature infants beginning in the first days of life were found to spend significantly more time engaged in cuddling and *en face* behaviors during feeding just preceding discharge than mothers who first handled their babies after 20 days of age (Kennell, Gordon, & Klaus 1970). Other studies indicate that early contact mothers engage in more holding and ventral contact at 1-week discharge and more ventral contact at 1-month postdischarge (Leifer et al. 1970; Leifer et al. 1972). Separation mothers often held their infants at some distance from them, while the early contact mothers more often held their infants cradled close to their body or on their chest or shoulder. Further, the contact mothers exhibited a pattern of looking at the infant, talking to the infant, and refraining from looking and talking to others more often than the separated mothers. Supplementary data reported for these contact and separated mothers indicate that early separation may be associated with a greater incidence of relinquishing custody of infants, greater incidence of divorce, and unsuccessful attempts at breast feeding. For instance, two of the mothers in the separated premature group relinquished custody of their infants after discharge from the hospital. Furthermore, six cases of divorce occurred in the sample with five of them being in the separated group and the other one in the contact group. This last finding suggests a striking correlation between giving birth to a premature infant and family stress, although the causal patterns have not yet been identified.

Finally, Fanaroff, Kennell, and Klaus (1972) have shown that maternal visiting for low birth weight infants is predictive of later maternal treatment of their infants. Among the mothers with a low visiting record, there was higher incidence of battered and failure-to-thrive infants than among the mothers who visited their low birth weight infants during the hospitalization period.

Although the effect of postpartum separation of mother and low birth weight infant has been emphasized in this section, it should be noted that separation may occur more frequently with different types of delivery, such as Caesarean sections. Possibly the early mother-infant separation that may accompany this type of delivery is, in part, responsible for Lenoski's (1974) recent finding that 30% of the abused children in his sample, in contrast to 3.2% of the nonabused children, were delivered by Caesarean section.

Overall, the findings reviewed above provide strong evidence to support the contention that the amount of early maternal involvement with infants has a significant influence on mothers' attitudes about their parenting role, their skill in caring for their infants, and patterns of social interactions with infants. In turn, these factors may, in part, account for the greater tendency of premature infants to become the victims of abuse. Perhaps, as Parke and O'Leary (1975) note, father-infant attachment would be enhanced as well with greater opportunities for paternal visiting during the early postpartum period. Similarly, if the father has the opportunity to learn and practice his caretaking skills during this period, he may be more likely to share with his wife in the caretaking of his infant. This may serve to relieve the mother of some of this responsibility and reduce the probability of tension-elicited abuse.

3. The Older Child's Role in Abuse

It is not just the infant that contributes to his own abuse; the child may elicit abuse from his caretakers at a variety of points throughout his development. In our earlier discussion, the child's role in escalating discipline was noted. In this section, some further examples of the role played by the child in his own abuse will be presented. As in infancy, the older child's appearance, general tempo, or style as well as his specific behavioral reactions are important factors.

Just as appearance of the infant may be an important determinant of the degree of attachment, and thereby may indirectly affect the probability of parental abuse of children, physical attractiveness can modify the disciplinary tactics that adults employ with older children. A recent study by Dion (1974) illustrates this relationship. Female adults viewed a videotape of an interaction between another adult and an ostensibly attractive or unattractive 8-year-old child. When given the opportunity to penalize the child for incorrect responses on a picture-matching task, the adults penalized the unattractive boy more than the attractive boy. The degree of punitiveness, then, may in part be determined by the physical attractiveness of the vicitm and, by implication, may affect the child's potential for abuse.

It is not merely physical attractiveness that determines disciplinary choices, but certain behavior patterns may be influential as well. Activity level is one pattern recently examined by Stevens-Long (1973) and is of particular interest because of the relationships between prematurity and later activity level patterns, and prematurity and abuse. Parents responded to videotapes of sequences depicting either an overactive, underactive, or an average-active child. The adults were required to select an appropriate disciplinary tactic (ranging from reward and affection to corporal punishment) when the child misbehaved at a number of points during the videotape sequence. More severe discipline was selected for the overactive child than for the underactive and average-active child. In summary, highly active children may elicit more extreme forms of discipline from their caretakers.

Another manner in which the child may contribute to the selection of severe disciplinary tactics is, of course, by his own reactions to being disciplined. In a recent examination of this issue, Parke, Sawin, and Kreling (1974) asked adults to monitor a child in a nearby room via a closed circuit videotape arrangement. The adults were to discipline the child whenever the child misbehaved; the reaction of the child to the adult discipline was systematically varied in one of the following ways: (1) the child ignores the adult, (2) the child makes reparation, (3) the child pleads with the adult, or (4) the child behaves in a defiant manner. When the child misbehaved on a future occasion, the adult disciplinary choice was affected by the child's prior reaction to being disciplined. The children who had reacted with defiance received the harshest discipline while those who had made a reparative response received less severe discipline. The implication of the study is clear: children's reactions in a disciplinary context can clearly modify adult behavior and may serve to maintain and/or increase adult punitiveness.

These brief examples demonstrate a clear relationship between child characteristics and behavior and adult punitiveness. In future research, closer attention needs to be paid to the role that the child may play in eliciting abusive reactions from his caretakers.

4. Summary

The child may contribute to his own abuse in a variety of ways. There may be some genetically determined physical and behavioral characteristics of the child that may predispose the child to abuse. Alternatively, the child may develop behaviors through interaction with parents and peers that make him a likely target for abuse. The infant as a target of abuse was discussed; abuse was viewed as an outcome of the demands that infants place on caretakers. Special attention was given to the low birth weight infant, who is particularly likely to be abused. Some of the characteristics of the low birth weight infant, including appearance and slow maturation, were viewed as contributing factors. In addition, mother-infant separation in the early postpartum period which may interfere with the development of mother-infant attachment was viewed as a further factor accounting for the abuse of the low birth weight infant. Finally, it was argued that the older child's appearance, temperament, and behavioral reactions to discipline may contribute to the development of parental abusive patterns.

V. CONTROL OF ABUSE

Control of child abuse can be viewed in short- and long-term perspectives. Short-term control involves some type of crisis intervention, which may prevent an imminent case of abuse from occurring. Telephone hot lines, crisis nurseries, and day-care drop-off centers are examples of short-term control. Similarly, temporary removal of the abused child from the home may be viewed as another form of short-term control.

However, in light of the large number of abused children reported annually, removal and placement cannot be viewed as an economically feasible solution to the abuse problem. Long-term control has the more ambitious aim of restructuring the social interaction patterns of the family members that may be the cause of abuse or the modification of either the child's or the parent's attitudes, values, personality, and/or behavior which are viewed as causing the abuse. The particular form that long-term intervention and control assume will vary with the idiosyncratic theoretical views of the intervention agent. Next we will examine the

implications of each of the three main approaches—psychiatric, sociological, and social-situational—for the control of abuse. Not all of these
possible control methods have been employed; however, it seems useful
to explore fully the range of techniques that could prove useful in the
planning of control programs. Finally, the existing programs will be reviewed, and some evaluation of their effectiveness will be offered.

A. PSYCHIATRIC APPROACH

To the extent that the psychiatric model of abuse focuses primarily on
the character and personality deficiencies of the parents, the main aim of
psychiatric treatment is the modification of parental personality. Psychiatric intervention can assume a variety of forms ranging from individual
psychotherapy to various types of group therapy, usually under the direction of a psychiatric or psychological professional. The recommended
form of therapeutic intervention varies widely across professionals.
Choices among therapies are probably as much a function of the prior
theoretical orientation of the therapist as a function of an examination of
the dynamics of the child abuse. Estimates concerning the success of
various forms of psychotherapy vary widely. Green (1973) estimates that,
with proper combined therapeutic modalities and under optimum conditions, about 80% of abusing parents can be rehabilitated. However, as
Blumberg (1974) has commented: "The truth must be faced realistically
that about 20 to 50 percent of all cases, depending on time, place and
facilities, are untreatable" (p. 27).

Perhaps the most thoroughly instituted and evaluated program of psychiatric intervention is the Steele-Pollock program in Denver, Colorado.
In their words:

Our method of study was clinical, patterned basically after the usual
methods of psychiatric diagnosis and therapeutic interviews with an attempt to reach as deeply as possible into the patient's personality. In
addition to the directly psychiatric procedure, great use was made of
interviews and home visits by our social worker, whereby information
could be obtained about general modes of living and of actual day-by-
day interactions between parents and between parents and child. Contacts were made not only with the attacking parent but also with the
spouse. This was often inevitable, as it was not always possible at first to
know who had attacked the child. Later such contacts were maintained
or instituted because the uncovering of problems in the marriage made it
obvious that treatment of both parents was highly desirable. Interviews,
usually rather informal, were held whenever possible with attacker's parents and other relatives, and occasionally we had the chance to see an
abusing mother with her own mother in a joint interview and to observe
their interaction. From such sources we obtained information which cor-

roborated, corrected, or elaborated with memories which the attacker had of his own childhood and upbringing. A battery of psychological tests was done on most of our attacking parents and in some instances, on the non-attacking spouse as well. [Steele & Pollock 1968, p. 105]

The duration of contact varied, with most parents being seen over a period of months and several for as long as 3–5 years. Some patients were hospitalized in the early stages of therapy, while other patients were seen on a regular basis of 1–3 times per week. One important feature was the continued availability of the therapist by telephone. These investigators reported that three-quarters of their 60 patients showed significant "improvement" which was defined as:

. . . when dangerously severe physical attack of the infant was eliminated and milder physical attack in the form of disciplinary punishment was either eliminated or reduced to a non-injurious minimum. Of equal significance was a reduction in demand upon and criticism of children accompanied by increased recognition of a child as an individual with age-appropriate needs and behavior. Further signs of improvement in the parents were increased abilities to relate to a wider social milieu for pleasureable satisfaction and source of help in time of need rather than looking to their children for such responses. We did not always try nor did we always succeed in making any change in all of the psychological conflicts and character problems of our patients. [Steele & Pollock 1968, p. 145]

Although the Denver program has successfully suppressed abusive behavior, the durability of the treatment effects has not been established. However, Pollock and Steele (1972) suggest that "the parents are not automatically protected from future trouble" (p. 21) as a result of therapeutic intervention and recommend that the parents be able to reinstitute contact in case of future crises.

Although the program developed from a traditional psychiatric model, the type of therapy is multifaceted and nonorthodox in many respects. In spite of the emphasis on modification of patient personality, considerable stress is placed on reprogramming the "basic pattern of child rearing." The use of home observations which permitted an assessment of the parent-child interaction patterns may have increased the success of these efforts to modify child rearing. In short, this was not an intervention program whose sole emphasis was on the modification of parental personality through the development of a positive patient-client relationship.

In evaluating the effectiveness of any intervention effort, the cost in parent and change-agent time and money needs to be carefully considered. Second, the practical utility of intervention programs must be evaluated in terms of the feasibility of wide-scale application to groups at both local and state or even national levels. Regardless of the eventual judgment concerning the effectiveness of individual psychotherapy as a treatment for child-abusing parents, there are serious practical limitations to this approach. The amount of therapist time, client time, and monetary outlay places severe limitations on the type of individuals for whom this technique can be used. Generally, this type of intervention will be restricted to the treatment of middle- and upper-class clients; in light of the apparent disproportionate number of lower-class abusers, the method must be viewed as one of limited wide-scale utility. In terms of state or national intervention, both cost and therapist availability make this approach unlikely.

B. SOCIOLOGICAL APPROACH

There are many implications for control that are derived from a sociological perspective. The most articulate spokesman for wide-ranging changes in societal values and the social structure is Gil (1970, 1974), who recently stated that "primary prevention of child abuse, on all levels, would require fundamental changes in social philosophy and value premises in societal institutions and in human relations" (Gil 1974, pp. 22–23). It would also require a reconceptualization of childhood, of children's rights, and of child rearing. It would necessitate rejecting the use of force as a means for achieving societal ends, especially in dealing with children. It would require the elimination of poverty and of alienating conditions of production, major sources of stress and frustration which tend to trigger abusive acts toward children in adult-child interaction. And, finally, it would necessitate the elimination of psychological illness.

Specifically, Gil has offered a number of general suggestions that are aimed to

unconditional elimination of poverty by assuring to all members of society, without discrimination, equal opportunity to the enjoyment of life through:

(*a*) adequate income derived from employment whenever feasible, or assured by means of a system of nonstigmatizing guaranteed-income maintenance based on legal entitlement rather than on charity and bureaucratic discretion;

(*b*) comprehensive health care and social services;

(*c*) decent and adequate housing and neighborhoods, free from the stigmatizing milieu and conditions of many existing public-housing programs;

(*d*) comprehensive education fitting inherent capacities and assuring the realization of each person's potential;

(*e*) cultural and recreational facilities. [Gil 1970, p. 145]

While few would argue with Gil's recommendations that the elimination of poverty should be a national priority, the extent to which this level of solution will aid in the reduction of child abuse is unknown. First, this general set of recommendations is based on the assumption that child abuse is a poverty-related phenomenon; earlier, we raised serious questions concerning whether this is, in fact, the case. To the extent that child abuse is a class-free phenomenon, this general solution deals only with a portion of the problem. Abuse still occurs in families where poverty is not a problem and source of stress. Even if Gil's analysis and recommendations are correct, they would require extensive supplementation to aid in the control of non-poverty-based abuse. Second, even if there is a link between poverty and abuse, can we necessarily assume that the reduction of poverty will result in abuse reduction? For example, possibly there are third-order factors which are related to both abuse and poverty which are, in fact, responsible for the apparent correlation. Third, Gil seems to be following a repeated tendency to blame any problem that poverty-level individuals may have on the low level of income; this is a solution that is recommended for nearly all of the problems of the poor. It is questionable whether these general solutions or panaceas are any longer adequate. Fourth, the solution is highly impractical; there can be general commitment to the elimination of poverty, but alternative solutions that are more practical to implement and more *specifically* related to the question of abuse per se would seem to be required.

Gil (1970) has made a series of more specific proposals that are more directly related to the analysis of child abuse. First, comprehensive family planning programs and legal medical abortions are recommended. Both of these suggestions flow from prior research which suggests that child abuse is more frequent in large families and in the case of unwanted children. Second, Gil recommends family-life education and counseling programs for both teenagers and adults that are aimed at providing realistic information concerning the tasks and demands of marriage and child rearing. This would serve to avoid the unrealistic expectations for children that characterize many abusive parents (cf. Steele & Pollock 1968). Another suggestion offered by Gil has been incorporated into many of the current child abuse control programs, namely, support services for mothers, which serve to relieve the stress of child care. The assumption underlying this suggestion is that "no mother should be expected to care for her children around the clock 365 days a year" (Gil 1970, p. 147). Specifically, Gil recommends:

A range of high quality, neighborhood-based social, child-welfare, and child-protective services geared to the reduction of environmental and internal stresses on family life, and especially on mothers who carry major responsibility for the child-rearing function. Such stresses are known to precipitate incidents of physical abuse of children, and any measure that would reduce these stresses would also indirectly reduce the incidence of child abuse. Family counseling, homemaker and house-keeping services, mother's helpers and baby-sitting services, family and group day-care facilities for preschool and school-age children are all examples of such services. [1970, p. 147]

These suggestions are well grounded in the prior sociological analysis and would appear to offer considerable promise for the control of child abuse. Programs, such as nursery schools and day-care centers, may serve not only to relieve parents of their child care responsibilities, but to provide an opportunity for the child to learn new patterns of social inter-action as a result of exposure to peers as well as a new set of adults. To the extent that the abusive behavior in some cases may be due to the child's behavior, opportunities for modifying child behavior patterns in these nonhome contexts may, in turn, alter the parent-child interaction patterns in the home situation. Specific techniques for the modification of child behavior will be discussed in the next section, which concerns the implications of the social situational approach for the control of abuse.

C. SOCIAL-SITUATIONAL APPROACH

There are certain distinctive features of a social-situational approach to the control of child abuse. First, it assumes that the cause of abuse is not in the individual, but in the social situation which, in turn, may be maintaining certain patterns of behavior. In contrast to a psychiatric approach which stresses modification of the verbal output of the "pa-tient" in a nonhome setting, this approach focuses on the modification of *observable behavior* in the home context. Therefore, the locus of change is the setting in which the abuse occurs; the content of the treatment is the actual observed behavior of the parent. Third, the assumption is that there is usually a high degree of interdependence between the abusing parent and the victim and, therefore, both parent and child must be treated; although for some phases of treatment the child and parent may be worked with separately, it is assumed that any separate changes in one partner will alter the behavior of the other partner in the dyad.

1. Techniques for the Modification of Child Behavior

As noted earlier in this chapter, children themselves sometimes may elicit abusive behavior from their caretakers by persisting in noxious and deviant behavior; it is in the service of attempting to control this undesir-able behavior that abuse may occur. Therefore, an examination of effec-tive tehniques for controlling children's behavior which avoid the use of punitive tactics that may tend to escalate to abusive levels is worthwhile.

First, a brief comment about punishment. Punishment can be an effective technique for controlling children's behavior, if it is carefully administered (Parke 1970). However, the effectiveness of punishment is dependent on a variety of parameters such as the timing, intensity, consistency of the punishing event, as well as the nature of the relationship between the punishing agent and the recipient of punishment (Parke 1972). While it would be possible to teach parents more effective ways of using punishment as a control tactic, physical punishment has a series of undesirable side effects which severely curtail its value as a technique of parental control (Parke 1972). As noted above, the punished child may model the behavior of the punitive parent and display increased aggression. A variety of studies (Ulrich 1966) have demonstrated that the pain associated with the administration of physical punishment may itself lead to an increase in aggression. Another undesirable consequence of punishment is the effect on the agent-child relationship. As a result of punishment, the child may be motivated to avoid the punishing parent. Consequently, the socialization agent may no longer be able to direct or influence the child's behavior. In a recent experimental study, Redd, Morris, and Martin (1975) demonstrated that children preferred work and play with adults who had previously treated them in a positive or neutral fashion and avoided a previously punishing adult. The implication is clear: punishment may be an effective modification technique, but the use of punishment by adults may lead the child to avoid that socializing agent and therefore undermine the adult's effectiveness as a future influence on the child's behavior.

Conditions such as crowded living arrangements often prevent the child from physically escaping the presence of the agent. Continued use of punishment in an inescapable context, however, may lead to passivity and withdrawal (Seligman, Maier, & Solomon 1969) or adaptation to the punishing stimuli themselves. In any case, whether escape is possible or not, the quality of the agent-child relationship may deteriorate if punishment is used with high frequency; punishment administered by such an agent will, therefore, be less effective in inhibiting the child.

The undesirable effects of physical punishment mentioned here probably occur mainly in situations where the disciplinary agents are indiscriminately punitive. In child-rearing contexts where the agent rewards and encourages a large proportion of the child's behavior, even though selectively and occasionally punishing certain kinds of behavior, these side effects are less likely to be found (Walters & Parke 1967).

There are many alternative techniques that can be employed to successfully control children's behavior that avoid the negative consequences of physical punishment. Extinction (Williams 1959), reinforcement of incompatible responses (Brown & Elliot 1965), time-out

(Hawkins et al. 1966), and verbal reasoning (Parke 1970, 1974) are effective techniques for improving parental control of children's behavior. Extinction involves the nonreinforcement of the undesirable response; in the study by Williams (1959), the crying behavior of an infant was diminished by systematically ignoring this behavior. The effectiveness of reinforcement of incompatible responses is illustrated in a study by Brown and Elliot (1965). Adults were instructed to ignore aggressive responses while rewarding cooperative behavior. Through these procedures, the amount of aggressive behavior was reduced. Another technique is "time-out," which involves the removal of the child from the situation for a brief time period. A number of investigators have demonstrated the usefulness of this control tactic for modification of deviant child behaviors in home situations. Hawkins et al (1966) trained mothers to use these procedures to control aggressive behavior. Risley and Baer (1973) discuss a variety of these behavior-modification techniques in detail. Finally, Parke (1974) has demonstrated that children's deviant behavior can be effectively inhibited by the provision of verbal rationales.

These techniques may be utilized by an outside therapist or change agent who can modify the child's behavior with the aim of reducing the deviant behavior that may be eliciting the punitive and possibly abusive behavior. However, it is assumed that abusive behavior of parents will be more adequately modified through a program of parental retraining. In the next section, techniques for modifying parental control tactics will be examined.

2. Techniques for the Modification of Parental Disciplinary Behavior

Programs for parental retraining have a two-level focus. First, the parents themselves who are using physically punitive tactics need to be provided with a new repertoire of training tactics that will be effective in child control and, therefore, be adopted by them to replace their punitive behavior. Second, through the use of these techniques, the child behaviors which may be eliciting highly punitive parental reactions will be altered. As noted above, social learning principles of operant conditioning have been utilized in the development of extremely effective techniques for modification of children's behavior, and, more recently, these same principles, in conjunction with modeling techniques (Bandura 1969), have been employed in developing strategies for the effective retraining of parents to employ nonpunitive control tactics.

To illustrate this approach to the modification of parent and child behaviors, we will examine a comprehensive program for the retraining of parents of aggressive children developed by Patterson (1974). This program is of particular relevance to child abuse since one-fourth of the parents in the program would be classified as abusive. This treatment program is based on social learning principles, particularly operant conditioning concepts, in which the relationships between parental reactions and deviant behavior are the focus. It is assumed that much deviant behavior is maintained by parental and peer reactions; therefore, by making the parents aware of these relationships and by giving them the opportunity to learn and rehearse alternative techniques for dealing with their children, the deviant behavior can be brought under better control. A number of steps are involved. First, the parents are required to study a programmed text on social learning–based child-management techniques. The book emphasizes that child behavior can be controlled and in nontechnical language explains social learning principles such as reinforcement, shaping, generalization, coercion, extinction, and punishment. The parents must complete the book before proceeding with the treatment. In the next phase of the program, the parents are taught to carefully define, track, and record a series of targeted deviant and/or prosocial child behaviors. This involves defining in a precise fashion the exact behavior, to note the elicitors and consequences that accompany a response, and, finally, to record the occurrences. During this phase they are monitored frequently by telephone.

The third stage involves a parent training group, where modeling and role-playing procedures are used to illustrate appropriate techniques. There are two aims in this phase: (1) to teach the parents to reinforce and encourage prosocial appropriate behaviors and (2) to reduce the rate of occurrence of deviant behaviors. To accomplish the first aim, the parents are taught to recognize and reinforce in a consistent way instances of acceptable behavior. The complementary set of procedures involves the use of time-out for deviant behavior. Time-out is a procedure whereby a child is removed for a specified period from the reinforcing environment and placed in isolation. Usually a bathroom is used for this purpose. This is an effective technique for reducing deviant behavior in children; moreover the parent, who may use more severe punitive techniques, is provided with alternative and effective procedures for child control. In group-training situations which consist of 3–4 sets of parents, these behavior management skills are directly modeled, and the novice parents engage in supervised role playing of these same skills. Usually 8–12 weekly sessions are sufficient. Where necessary, training sessions are conducted in the home with the experimenters modeling the appropriate parenting skills. A final aspect of the program consists of learning to construct contracts which specified contingencies for a list of problem behaviors occurring at home and/or at school. In addition, Patterson combines these procedures with a set of classroom interventions.

To assess the effectiveness of the program, detailed observations by trained observers of the interaction patterns between the parents and the deviant child are made in the home situation. A careful assessment of 27 families indicated that there was a significant decrease in deviant behavior from the baseline across the treatment phase. Follow-up assessments revealed that there was an increase in noxious behavior for half of the families during the month following the cessation of treatment; however, by providing families with a "booster shot" of approximately 2 hours of extra treatment, the deviant behavior was reduced. Most important, the results suggest that the effects induced by the training were relatively stable over 1 year. Finally, in contrast to long-term psychiatric therapy, this type of intervention program was relatively economical: the cost in terms of therapist contact time was 31.4 hours for the family training intervention.

The success of this program is impressive and clearly documents the feasibility of retraining parents to use nonpunitive modification tactics for effective child control. Part of the reason for the long-term stability of the changes is that, as the child's behavior improves, the relationship between parent and child may improve and the negative attitude to the child may diminish. The child may become a more attractive and valued family member and, as such, a less likely target for abuse.

These effects have been partially replicated by Johnson et al. (1974). Based on the fact that some of these families were abusive, there is an indication that these procedures are applicable to the modification of abusive parental behaviors. Recently, a child abuse intervention program in Los Angeles (Savino & Sanders 1973) adopted a social learning approach in retraining parents and is utilizing the Patterson and Guillon text, *Living with Children* (1968). Whether exposure to social learning principles through the text alone, without the extensive modeling and role-playing components that are part of the full-scale Patterson program, will be effective remains unknown without careful follow-up documentation of the success rate of this program.

The Patterson program should serve as a model for future intervention attempts in terms of the careful assessment, programmatic intervention, and detailed documentation of outcomes. The Patterson work illustrates that it is possible to introduce adequate assessment and evaluation procedures as part of an intervention program in this area.

3. Techniques for Anger Control

Another approach recognizes the fact that not all parental abusive behavior is, in fact, due to annoying and disruptive behavior of a child; many other sources of frustration may be present in the environment, and an examination of techniques for lessening anger in the face of potentially anger-eliciting stimuli is useful. What techniques are useful for anger control?

A number of techniques have been suggested including (*a*) reinforcement of nonangry responses, (*b*) role playing and modeling of nonangry reactions, and (*c*) desensitization in the presence of the anger-evoking stimuli.

An early study by Davitz (1952) illustrates the role of reinforcement in the anger-reduction process. In this experiment, children were reinforced for either nonangry cooperative responses or angry aggressive reactions; when they were subsequently frustrated by an adult, the children who had previously been reinforced for their nonangry cooperative behavior reacted with little anger and aggression relative to the other children who were encouraged for their angry responses. Clearly, reactions to frustration can be modified by reinforcement of alternative, nonangry responses. Using a related approach, Mahoney (1971) directly rewarded hyperaggressive boys for remaining calm and noncombative in the face of peer harassment. The magnitude of the rewards varied in relation to the length of time that the victim was able to maintain his composure and equanimity.

Just as parental behaviors can be reprogrammed successfully through the use of modeling and role-playing techniques, anger reactions in the face of frustrating and other anger-eliciting cues can often be modified by the use of these same techniques. The assumption underlying this approach is that new, alternative nonangry modes of reacting in anger-eliciting situations can be learned successfully by exposure to models who demonstrate these new reactions. Second, it is assumed that the observer needs practice and rehearsal of these new behaviors, and if these new behaviors are rewarded, the reactions become a habitual part of the response repertoire. As Bandura (1973) has noted: "Given adequate demonstration, guided practice and success experiences, this method is almost certain to produce favorable results" (p. 253).

Gittelman (1965) has successfully employed these techniques in modifying the aggressive-angry reactions of children. After constructing a hierarchy of annoying situations, the children then enacted these situations and rehearsed nonviolent tactics for handling them. This type of anger-control tactic will probably be most effective when combined with an extensive modeling component which involves exposure to a wide range of models who demonstrate nonaggressive and nonangry solutions to conflictful and frustrating problems. Chittenden (1942) also has demonstrated the usefulness of modeling and rehearsal in modifying aggressive behavior in children. More recently, modeling and behavioral rehearsal techniques have been applied to the modification of anger in adults. Rimm et al. (1974) successfully treated males who had a history of expressing anger in an anti-social manner. These investigators employed group assertive training, which involves the modeling and rehearsal of appropriate nonaggressive solutions to a potentially anger-eliciting problem.

Another technique for anger control is desensitization by which the anger-evoking stimuli lose some of their anger-eliciting potency. Herrell (1971) successfully employed this technique in a chronically assaultive adult. By providing relaxation instructions while the person imagined the anger-eliciting scenes, the anger reactions were reduced.

The comparative effectiveness of these different approaches for anger control merits investigation in future research. Similarly, the effectiveness of these techniques in modifying the angry reactions of abusive adults needs to be examined.

4. Techniques for Increasing Social Contacts

One of the characteristics of abusive adults is their isolation from other members of the community. In a series of recent studies, modeling techniques have been successfully employed in the modification of social isolation behavior. There are two assumptions underlying this research: (1) the social isolate may be fearful of other individuals and/or (2) the isolate may lack the necessary social skills to successfully initiate and maintain social contacts. These techniques have been successfully applied to both children and adults. O'Conner (1969) exposed children who displayed extreme social withdrawal, characterized by isolation from both adults and other children, to a film of a child interacting with other individuals. The film model gradually increased the degree of social interaction as the film progressed. In contrast to a control film of nonsocial behavior, the children exposed to the experimental film increased their degree of subsequent social participation. With adults, McFall and Twentyman (1972) have employed a combination of modeling and behavioral rehearsal to overcome shyness and increase social assertiveness in young men. Rimm and Masters (1974) have presented a comprehensive review of the application of modeling techniques to the modification of social deficits. These techniques could be extremely useful for modifying the social isolation that often characterizes abusive adults. By teaching them new social skills, they will be better able to form friendships and seek social support in crisis situations.

5. Increasing the Awareness of Harmful Effects

Another tactic that is probably most effectively employed in conjunction with modeling and behavioral rehearsal techniques involves increasing the awareness of the harmful effects of abusive behavior. Some abusive parents tend to minimize the harm that they have caused. As a first step in sensitizing them to the impact of their behavior, vivid videotape and film displays of both abused and battered children as well as depictions of different adults abusing their children could be shown. These films would have to be accompanied by commentary which highlights the unjustifiability of this behavior and which underlines the negative, harmful outcomes for the children. Note that two components are involved here: first, an increased sensitivity to the harmful effects of excessive physical treatment and, second, the explicit labeling of the observed outcome as "bad" and unjustified. This latter labeling may serve to undermine some parental attempts to justify their behavior in light of higher-order disciplinary principles.

In part, both the specific teaching of new control tactics and the modification of attitudes involve the induction of new norms and standards that were not learned during their own socialization.

6. Summary

In this section the implications of each of the three main approaches—psychiatric, sociological, and social-situational—for the control of abuse were presented. Under the psychiatric model, individual and group therapy has been utilized to modify the behavior of abusive parents. From a sociological perspective, on the other hand, a variety of recommendations aimed at the alleviation of stress induced by poverty conditions were discussed. Support services for mothers, such as day-care centers and homemaker programs, would seem to offer particular promise. Next, the implications of the social-situational model for the control of abuse were examined. Techniques for nonpunitive management of children's behavior were discussed as well as ways of training parents to utilize these alternative tactics. Approaches for increasing anger control in abusive adults were examined, as well as techniques for the modification of the pattern of social isolation that characterizes many abusive families.

D. CURRENT INTERVENTION PROGRAMS

In this section, we will outline a variety of current innovative programs and services which have been developed to attempt to control child abuse. These are supplements to a wide network of state and local welfare and social work agencies and child protection services which have traditionally handled abuse and neglect problems; these traditional approaches are reviewed elsewhere (Davoren 1974; Glazier 1971; Kempe & Helfer 1972). There are a number of different types of intervention pro-

TABLE 3

Current Intervention Programs

Name of Program Location and Date Begun	Individual Psychotherapy with a Psychiatrist, Psychologist, or Social Worker	Individual Lay Therapy or Parent Aide	Group Therapy or Parent Groups	Child-Care Instruction	Day-Care Crisis Nursery	Medical Care	24-Hour Hotline	Research Prof. Training Public Education
Kentucky Welfare Dept. Protective Services, Louisville, 1958........	Casework with social worker		Parent group led by social worker mtgs. twice/ month	Child care taught in parent mtgs.				
University of Colorado Med. Ctr., Child Abuse Study, Denver, 1962..	With psychiatrist 1–3 times/ week + social worker						Staff accessible 24 hours	Research prof. training public education
Massachusetts Dept. of Pub. Welfare Div. of Child Guardianship, Boston, 1967..........	Casework with social worker				1971-est. day-care program			
Parents' Center Project, Boston, 1968..........	Home visits by social worker on request		Group therapy led by social worker once/week		Day-care program	For children 6 mos.– 3 yrs.		Research prof. training

Mothers Anonymous (Parents Anonymous), Redondo Beach, Calif., 1970.........	Individual relationship with another member possible	Group meetings led by member once/week		Self-referral hotline + members call each other	
C.A.L.M. (Child Abuse Listening Mediation), Santa Barbara, Calif., 1970.........	Volunteer lay therapists			2 nonprof. directors take calls	Community Education
UCLA, Neuropsychiatric Inst., Child Abuse Project, Los Angeles, 1971.........		Groups led by "surrogate parents" once/week	Child care in in group mtgs. lessons at home on request		Research
P.S.S. (Parental Stress Service), Berkeley, 1972	Volunteer lay therapists		Volunteers will baby-sit	Volunteers take calls	

TABLE 3 (*Continued*)

Name of Program Location and Date Begun	Individual Psychotherapy with a Psychiatrist, Psychologist, or Social Worker	Individual Lay Therapy or Parent Aide	Group Therapy or Parent Groups	Child-Care Instruction	Day-Care Crisis Nursery	Medical Care	24-Hour Hotline	Research Prof. Training Public Education
Children's Trauma Ctr., Oakland, Calif., 1972...	Available		Group, family, marital counsel			Special trauma clinic & follow up	Staff accessible 24 hrs.	Prof. train. community education
Child Protection Team Univ. of Colorado Med. Ctr., Denver, 1972		Lay therapists make 1–2 visits/week	"Families anony-mous", semi-self-help group	Homemaker & visiting nurse available	Crisis nursery		Prof. take calls	Research prediction prof. train. public education
S.C.A.N. (Suspected Child Abuse & Neglect), Little Rock, Ark., 1972	Intensive supportive therapy	Lay therapists			Day-care & crisis nursery			
Child Abuse Project, Maricopa County Hospital, Phoenix, 1973	Some individual counseling	Lay therapists	Group therapy led by volunteer		Crisis nursery	Medical care if parents accept soc. serv.	Volunteers take calls	Public education

C.A.P.E. (Child Abuse Prevention Effort), Philadelphia, 1973.....		Anonymous parent groups led by professional once/week		Professional volunteers take calls	Research public educ.
S.P.S. (Spotlight on Parental Stress) Oakland, Calif., 1973..	Volunteer lay therapists			Crisis phone	
Family Focus, Birmingham, Ala., 1973	Family aids		Through nursery schools	Listening service supervised by prof.	Speaker on money management
CALL (Child Abuse Listening Service), Santa Monica, Calif., 1974.............	Makes referrals to parent group or Child Trauma Prevention Program at UCLA			Listening service	

gram such as a parent group or counseling service. The types of person-grams that merit distinction: (1) parent groups which provide group discussion and support for child-abusing parents, (2) home support personnel who provide assistance in the home environment, (3) crisis services such as hotlines, (4) drop-off nurseries and day-care centers, (5) childcare instruction, and (6) public education. Typically, intervention programs have one or more of these different approaches represented as the outline of current programs in table 3 indicates.

1. Parent's Groups

Parent groups provide child abusers with the opportunity to meet others with similar problems and feelings to discuss personal experiences relating to themselves, their children, and their marriage. Meetings are usually held weekly for 2 hours, and may be with or without a professional leader. Group members report that they profit from the helpfulness of knowing that other people have problems and feelings similar to their own (McFerran 1958). Another positive aspect of parent groups is the opportunity for meaningful social experience for otherwise isolated people (Feinstein, Paul, & Esmiol 1964). No systematic assessment of the effectiveness of this approach is available.

Parents Anonymous is a self-help group which maintains independence from professional help. An attempt is made in the meetings to help one another by presenting positive behavioral alternatives to problem situations such as child abuse. Group cohesiveness is fostered by members using each other for support and guidance, helping each other without judgment, moralization, or stigma (Parents Anonymous 1972). Group members share phone numbers and are encouraged to contact each other any time for relief of stress or to report positive experiences. Kempe and Helfer (1972) have offered a series of suggestions for strengthening these self-help group programs, including: (1) the development of group intervention skills for the session leaders; (2) affiliation with a hospital or community-based child abuse consultation team as a backup resource for special cases; (3) assistance in providing child-rearing education for members; (4) a follow-through program for drop-outs; and (5) a program to aid parents in improving their relationships with their children.

Parent group programs with professional leadership may use the model of surrogate parent leaders. A child abuse program at UCLA uses two surrogate parent co-therapists, a male clinical psychologist and a female psychiatric nurse (Paulson & Chaleff 1973; Savino & Sanders 1973). The surrogate parent model is seen as useful for work with abusing parents since it facilitates identification and modeling of parent surrogate roles.

2. Home Support Programs

Parent Aides, one of the most innovative recent intervention programs, was developed by Kempe and Helfer (1972) as an off-shoot of the highly successful "foster grandparent program" sponsored by OEO in the 1960s. This parent aide program is a lay therapist intervention effort whose participants function as family friends for abusing parents. In contrast to the typical social worker load of 15–30 cases, an aid is assigned to only one or two families. Their main function is to provide advice and support for the family over an extended period of 8–12 months on a regular basis, usually in the parents' home. The aide is always available by phone 24 hours a day, 7 days a week, and the parent is encouraged to make use of the aide, especially during a crisis. Attempts are made to match aides and families by race, education, and social and economic class on the assumption that this similarity would facilitate family acceptance of the aide's intervention. The focus of the aide's work is the parents and their problem; the child is viewed as secondary. In the Kempe-Helfer program the parent aides receive support and advice through bi-weekly group therapy sessions as well as ongoing supervision by a social worker.

How successful has the program been? Unfortunately, no statistical data are available to date, but "clinical results have been outstandingly good at a fraction of the cost of employing psychiatrists and social workers as therapists" (Kempe & Helfer 1972, p. 44).

The homemaker service can serve the function of relieving the mother and/or sharing with the mother the responsibility of managing the children and the household duties. A number of agencies have employed these homemakers, but, again, data concerning their effectiveness are lacking.

3. Hotline Services

Using the successful model of emergency telephone lines for suicide cases as a guide, hotlines for potential child abusers have expanded rapidly in the last few years. The public is made aware of these 24-hour emergency hotlines for potential or actual child abusers through a variety of media including radio, TV, billboards, and newspapers. A newspaper ad sponsored by the CALM program states: "Is your child abused, neglected? Let us share your problems. Keep CALM in mind, call . . . for help" (Pike 1973). The aim of the hotlines is generally twofold. First, through the availability of support in a crisis situation, the hotline service aims to prevent abuse before it occurs. Second, it serves as a referral agency for either potential or actual abusing parents and attempts to encourage parental involvement in some type of more long-range pro-

nel staffing the hotlines as well as the types of referral vary widely across the country. Some programs use trained volunteers for hotlines while others use only professionals for hotline work and volunteers as lay therapists.

4. Crisis Nurseries and Drop-off Centers

Crisis nurseries provide the parent in a crisis situation with 24-hour emergency short-term care for infants. Crisis nurseries originated because of the frequent observation that a major contributing factor to child abuse is the escalation of the parents' stress when faced with the task of caring for their children with no relief from those responsibilities. The Denver program's crisis nursery includes admission of the mother and infant "rooming in" fashion, so that the mother can be helped to develop parenting skills (Kempe & Helfer 1972; National Center for the Prevention and Treatment of Child Abuse and Neglect 1973). Another closely related service is the drop-off day-care center, which permits an older child to be left under professional supervision at times when the parent is under stress.

5. Child-Care Instruction

Since many abusive parents have been found to share common misunderstandings about child rearing (Spinetta & Rigler 1972), instruction in child rearing and normal child development are included in several programs. In some programs child care is taught in parent group meetings while in other programs it is taught individually in the home. Emphasis is on the practical aspects of child care such as toilet training and discipline. The UCLA child abuse program offers home instruction in behavior modification, teaching the parents the principles of reinforcement. A closely related project in Seattle (Slaby 1974), stressing similar principles of behavior management through the use of positive reinforcement, provides parent training through supervised practice of child-management techniques in a clinic setting. Early results indicate that this program is a promising approach; in fact, Slaby (1974, personal communication) reports that the program has been effective even when other group intervention efforts, such as "Parents Anonymous" have failed to modify parental behavior.

6. Public Education

Another service of child abuse programs is public education, which is aimed at increasing public awareness and knowledge concerning the scope and nature of child abuse. In addition to lectures, pamphlets, and films on child abuse, some programs provide information on the problems of normal parenting. For example, CALM offers a film-discussion program to adolescents in high school, which aims to expose future parents to some of the realities and responsibilities of parenthood. In view of the fact that most adolescents have a vague and unrealistic conception of the parental role, this type of public education is extremely valuable.

7. The Effectiveness of Current Intervention Programs

Although there have been many claims on behalf of these various intervention efforts, there has been insufficient systematic evaluation of the effectiveness of these different programs. Two strategies are necessary. First, the current programs need to introduce an evaluation component as part of their ongoing intervention effort. Second, a specific series of field-experimental intervention programs need to be established. These programs should include a systematic introduction of various types of intervention strategies both singly and in combination. Evaluation would be an integral part of this effort whereby abuse rates would be assessed at time points before, during, and after treatment to document the impact of the program. Then we would know not only which aspects of current programs are critical, but also the optimal combination of services that are most effective. Evaluation should not be restricted only to the treatment sample and the formal control groups, but should include assessments of other groups of parents in the community to determine the secondary effects of introducing abuse-control programs into a community on such issues as knowledge of abuse, attitudes toward abuse, readiness to report abusing adults, and, of course, rates of actual child abuse.

One approach to program assessment would involve the use of comparable counties as units for introducing different types of programs. With careful baseline assessments and follow-up evaluation, the relative effectiveness of various approaches could be determined. It is to be hoped that these evaluations would permit some conclusions concerning the relative effectiveness not only of various newly instituted child abuse programs but also provide some evaluation of their success in comparison to more traditional social service work approaches to this problem.

In future research, a clear distinction needs to be made between the functions and possibly the clientele served by different types of programs or program components. Short-term crisis intervention procedures such as hotlines and drop-off child-care centers need to be distinguished from long-term programs which aim to effect substantial changes in child-rearing practices. Both are probably necessary, but little is known about the relative impact of these different levels of intervention, nor is there information concerning the types of individuals which are best served by these different approaches. The general question concerning the criteria for matching intervention programs for different types of abusers needs serious attention.

Another issue concerns the type of parents who are consumers of these new innovative programs. Are they the same types of adults that would usually be seen by Social Welfare Services or are they a new breed of adults who otherwise would remain undetected since they are middle class and, therefore, unlikely to use community welfare agencies. For example, CALM has reported a self-referral rate of 61% in 1973—a figure which is significantly higher than the self-referral rate in most city and state welfare agencies. In short, it is not clear whether the rate of detection of abusers has shifted to include new individuals or whether the same types of clientele are merely using different sources of assistance. With increasingly sophisticated reporting centers, some evaluation of the secular shifts in the type of clientele that are being serviced by different types of programs may be possible.

While these increases in self-referral are encouraging, they raise a serious issue concerning the role of client-motivation variables in these programs. If the majority of parents who participate in child abuse programs are self-selected volunteers, they may have already made a commitment to alter their abusive behavior prior to the onset of the program. Although they may not change without assistance from the intervention program, they are probably more willing to comply with the demands of the program that are critical for behavior alteration than unmotivated parents. A number of therapists have noted the importance of client motivation in determining the success of an intervention program. For example, Moorehead (1970), in describing the key element of successful treatment of parents in a London child abuse program, stated that, once the parents can ask for and receive help, the vicious circle which leads to a battered child may be broken. Galdston (1971), reporting the outcome of the Parent's Center Project's recruitment of families, mentions that of the 42 families referred to the project, 19 withdrew before or after the intake interview. He readily acknowledges the motivation factor of the 23 families who remained in the program stating, "thus our parents appear to be the most motivated" of the initial group (p. 342), The critical issue is this: if current programs are successful, to what extent is their success due to the overrepresentation of motivated parents? While these new programs may prove to be valuable for abuse control, the effectiveness of these efforts may not be generalizable to unmotivated parents.

It is clear that careful, systematic evaluation of both programs and their clientele is urgently required to determine whether these programs are, in fact, fulfilling their goals of successful modification of abusive parental behavior.

8. Prediction of Abuse

One other recent innovation in the area of child abuse concerns prediction. There have been two recent attempts at a priori prediction of child abuse. Kempe (1973) reported an ongoing project in Aberdeen, Scotland, of postpartum prediction of child abuse. Data are collected by health visitors who systematically visit every home in the city to assist mothers in caring for their new infants. To identify potentially abusive mothers, the nurses ask a short set of questions concerning the maternal attitudes and feeding of their 8-week-old infant. The following are examples of the types of questions:

1. Does your baby cry excessively and does it make you feel like crying?
2. Do you dislike having somebody watch you feed the baby or take care of this baby?
3. Does your older child know when you're upset and does she take care of you at this time?

They then study every child in the city that has an accident or fails to thrive. Kempe writes, "I can tell you now that people who are going to have children who have accidents, inflicted or otherwise, answer these questions very differently from matched controls who enter the study because they had a child born the same day who had not had an accident." And once you identify a family that is at risk, you can successfully intervene (Kempe 1973). Unfortunately, systematic statistical reports of the results of this study are not yet available.

Another prediction attempt is being executed by the Denver Child Protection Team to establish criteria for identifying and helping mothers who appear to be at risk and unable to make positive healthy attachments to their children. Screening of pregnant women begins in the Ob-Gyn Clinic. Women who have unreasonable levels of expectation toward newborns and who seem to have problems with basic "mother-crafting" are observed during labor, delivery, and in the postpartum period. If it is felt that the mother is "high risk," she is randomly placed in one of two groups: an intervene group or a nonintervene group. The hospital contacts are documented and success of intervention is measured by the mother's ability to utilize intensive follow-up care (National Center for the Prevention and Treatment of Child Abuse and Neglect 1973).

Again, no data are available on the predictive success of this program; however, in light of our earlier discussions concerning the early mother-infant interaction context as a setting in which abusive patterns may develop, this approach appears to be well founded and promising. These prediction studies are among the most important recent innovations in the area of child abuse. If they are successful in identifying potential abusive caretakers, education programs for parents can begin immediately after birth and, hopefully, short-circuit the development of patterns of interaction which may lead to later abuse. Moreover, it is probably easier to prevent the development of these patterns of interaction than to modify them after they have been well established.

It is likely that there will be a considerable risk of overprediction in studies of abuse prediction. The problem of prediction in the area of child abuse has a conceptual and statistical parallel in another area that shares the common characteristics of being (*a*) low in frequency among the population and (*b*) multiply determined. Perhaps the best parallel to use to illustrate the problems of prediction comes from the closely related issue of the prediction of adult interpersonal violence. These studies addressed the question of whether it is possible to predict recidivism among parolees with a history of interpersonal violent offenses. In one attempt to predict violence, Kosol, Boucher, and Garofalo (1972) used a wide range of clinical and psychological measures as well as a "meticulous reconstruction of the family history elicited from multiple sources—the patient himself, his family, friends, neighbors, teachers, and employers and court, correctional and mental hospital records" (p. 383), and the percentage of false prediction was high. Only one-third of those predicted actually committed an act of violence, while 65% did not. As Monahan (1973) concluded after a careful review of the violence prediction studies: "Of those predicted to be dangerous, between 65% and 99% are false positives . . . violence is vastly overpredicted whether simple behavioral indicators are used or sophisticated multivariate analyses are employed and whether psychological tests are administered or thorough psychiatric examinations are performed. . . . The fact that even in these groups, with higher base rates for violence than the general population, violence cannot be validly predicted bodes very poorly for predicting violence among those who have not committed a criminal act" (1973, p. 8). Since these studies were aimed at detection of repeaters, it is assumed that the current attempts at the prediction of potentially abusive, but currently nonabusive, parents may be even more difficult. In light of the probable high rate of overprediction, an intervention program would have to be sufficiently broadly based so that all participants would benefit from the program—regardless of whether or not they would have actually abused their children at some later date. The types of education programs for child care and child rearing aimed at high-risk adolescent mothers would probably be suitable. The recent "infant stimulation" program initiated by Badger, Elass, and Sutherland (1974) at the Cincinnati General Hospital is prototypic of this approach; young teenage mothers are recruited during their hospital stay to attend weekly group discussion classes which are aimed at teaching mothers how to interact with and stimulate their infants. This type of program serves to provide important information about normal infant development which serves to correct unrealistic expectations and, second, through direct instruction, role playing, and modeling, the mothers learn to be effective caretakers.

9. Summary

A series of innovative intervention programs which are currently operating were examined. These include lay group therapy programs, homemaker services, emergency hotlines, crisis nurseries, as well as child-rearing and public education programs. Although these approaches are promising, no formal assessments concerning the effectiveness of these programs are available. Finally, some of the recent prediction attempts were described and the difficulties associated with successful prediction were discussed.

VI. EPILOGUE

It is clear that much has been learned since Kempe's classic paper in 1962 brought the problem of child abuse to national attention. A number of issues are still to be addressed if significant progress is to be made in future research in this area. The most pressing need at present is for greater concern for rigorous evaluation and assessment of all facets of the child abuse problem.

First, the interaction patterns among family members in abusive families need to be carefully observed and compared with nonabusive families to determine whether distinctive patterns can be isolated. These assessments should include husband-wife, sib-sib, as well as parent-child interaction patterns. Similar types of observational investigations need to be executed in nonhome settings to determine whether children in abusive families show different patterns in their interactions with peers and other adults. These observational studies should by supplemented by other assessment techniques, such as structured family intervention, to permit a closer examination of the decision-making strategies and problem-solving strategies of abusive and nonabusive families. Of particular urgency is the extensive investigation of middle-class as well as lower-class families. Whether the conditions that give rise to abuse are similar or different across social classes is a problem that merits much closer examination.

While new innovative programs spring up across the country in reaction to the increased awareness of the problem of child abuse, too little attention is paid to a careful evaluation of the short- and long-term impact of these programs. Recent methodological advances in evaluation research (Campbell 1969) permit meaningful, but unobtrusive, assessment of the impact of action-oriented intervention programs. To supplement already established efforts, carefully designed field intervention experiments are badly needed in which comparable areas of the country receive different types of programs. By comparing the rates of child abuse in the different areas, we will be able more adequately to determine the effectiveness of various types of intervention efforts. Without this type of systematic experimental intervention, little solid information will be available on which to make policy decisions for the establishment of statewide and countrywide programs of abuse control. In addition, considerable work is required to evaluate the effectiveness of a variety of group and individual intervention strategies, such as programs for modification of parental disciplinary tactics and for improving anger control of abusive parents.

The same criteria that are applied to the descriptive studies and the intervention programs hold for the prediction studies. While these appear promising, careful evaluation of the predictive accuracy is necessary if these procedures are to be refined and improved.

The best interests of children will be served only to the extent that the problem of child abuse is viewed, not just as a human tragedy, but also as a problem that is amenable to careful and rigorous research and analysis. Only through better understanding of the problem will we be better able to protect our children.

REFERENCES

Adelson, L. Slaughter of the innocents. *New England Journal of Medicine*, 1961, *264*, 1345–1 349.

Allen, H. D.; Ten Bensel, R. W.; & Raile, R. B. The battered child syndrome. *Minnesota Medicine*, 1968, *51*, 1793–1799.

Badger, E.; Elsass, S.; & Sutherland, J. M. Mother training as a means of accelerating childhood development in a high risk population. Unpublished manuscript, University of Cincinnati, 1974.

Bakan, D. *Slaughter of the innocents.* San Francisco: Jossey-Bass, 1971.

Bandura, A. Influence of model's reinforcement contingencies on the acquisition of imitative responses. *Journal of Personality and Social Psychology*, 1965, *1*, 589–595.

Bandura, A. The role of modeling processes in personality development. In W. W. Hartup & L. Smothergill (Eds.), *The young child: reviews of research.* Washington, D. C.: National Association for the Education of Young Children, 1967.

Bandura, A. *Principles of behavior modification.* New York: Holt, Rinehart & Winston, 1969.

Bandura, A. *Aggression: a social learning analysis.* New York: Prentice-Hall, 1973.

Baron, R. A. Magnitude of victim's pain cues and level of prior anger arousal as determinants of adult aggressive behavior. *Journal of Personality and Social Psychology*, 1971, *17*, 236–243.

Baron, R. M. The SRS model as a predictor of Negro responsiveness to reinforcement. *Journal of Social Issues*, 1970, *26*, 61–82.

Becker, T. T. Presentation to the American Medical Association, New York City, June 25, 1973.

Bell, R. Q. A reinterpretation of the direction of effects in studies of socialization. *Psychological Review*, 1968, *75*, 81–95.

Bell, R. Q. Contributions of human infants to caregiving and social interaction. In M. Lewis & L. A. Rosenblum (Eds.), *The effect of the infant on its caregiver.* New York: Wiley, 1974.

Bell, S. M., & Ainsworth, M. D. Infant crying and maternal responsiveness. *Child Development*, 1972, *43*, 1171–1190.

Bellak, L., & Antell, M. An intercultural study of aggressive behavior on children's playgrounds. *American Journal of Orthopsychiatry*, 1974, *44*, 503–511.

Berkowitz, L. *Aggression: a social psychological analysis.* New York: McGraw-Hill, 1962.

Berkowitz, L. Frustrations, comparisons, and other sources of emotional arousal as contributors to social unrest. *Journal of Social Issues*, 1972, *28*, 77–91.

Berkowitz, L. Some determinants of impulsive aggression: role of mediated associations with reinforcements for aggression. *Psychological Review*, 1974, *81*, 165–176.

Bernal, M. E.; Duryee, J. S.; Pruett, H. L.; & Burns, B. J. Behavior modification and the brat syndrome. *Journal of Consulting and Clinical Psychology*, 1968, *32*, 447–455.

Birns, B.; Blank, M.; & Bridger, W. H. The effectiveness of various soothing techniques on human neonates. *Psychomatic Medicine*, 1966, *28*, 316–322.

Birrell, R. G., & Birrell, J. H. W. The maltreatment syndrome in children: a hospital survey. *Medical Journal of Australia*, 1968, *2*, 1023–1029.

Blumberg, M. L. Psychopathology of the abusing parent. *American Journal of Psychotherapy*, 1974, *28*, 21–29.

Boardman, H. E. A project to rescue children from inflicted injuries. *Social Work*, 1962, *7*, 43–51.

Brett, D. I. *The battered and abused child syndrome.* Berkeley: University of California Press, 1967.

Brock, R. C., & Buss, A. H. Effects of justification for aggression and communication with the victim on postaggression dissonance. *Journal of Abnormal and Social Psychology*, 1964, *68*, 403–412.

Bronfenbrenner, U. Socialization and social class through time and space. In E. E. Baccoby, T. M. Newcomb, & E. L. Hartley (Eds.), *Readings in social psychology.* New York: Holt, 1958.

Brooks, V., & Hochberg, J. A psychophysical study of "cuteness." *Perceptual and Motor Skills*, 1960, *11*, 205.

Brown, P., & Elliott, R. The control of aggression in a nursery school class. *Journal of Experimental Child Psychology*, 1965, *2*, 103–107.

Bryant, H. D.; Billingsley, A.; Kerry, G. A.: Leefman, W. V.; Merrill, E. J.; Senecal, G. R.; & Walsh, B. G. Physical abuse of children—an agency study. *Child Welfare*, 1963, *42*, 125–130.

Buss, A. H. *The psychology of aggression.* New York: Wiley, 1961.

Buss, A. H. The effect of harm on subsequent aggression. *Journal of Experimental Research in Personality*, 1966, *1*, 249–255.

Calhoun, J. B. Population density and social pathology. *Scientific American*, 1962, *206*,

139–150.

Cameron, J. M.; Johnson, H. R. M.; & Camps, F. E. The battered child syndrome. *Medicine, Science and the Law*, 1966, *6*, 2–21.

Campbell, D. T. Reforms as experiments. *American Psychologist*, 1969, *24*, 409–429.

Caputo, D. V., & Mandell, W. Consequences of low birth weight. *Developmental Psychology*, 1970, *3*, 363–383.

Chittenden, G. E. An experimental study in measuring and modifying assertive behavior in young children. *Monographs of the Society for Research in Child Development*, 1942, *7*, (1, Serial No. 31).

Cochrane, W. A. The battered child syndrome. *Canadian Journal of Public Health*, 1965, *56*, 193–196.

Collias, N. E. The analysis of socialization in sheep and goats. *Ecology*, 1965, *37*, 228–239.

Committee of Investigation into Allegations of Neglect and Maltreatment of Young Children. Report to the Honorable the Chief Secretary and the Honorable the Minister of Health. Melbourne: Chelsea House, December 1967.

Curtis, G. Violence breeds violence. *American Journal of Psychiatry*, 1963, *120*, 386–387.

Davitz, J. R. The effects of previous training on postfrustration behavior. *Journal of Abnormal and Social Psychology*, 1952, *47*, 309–315.

Davoren, E. The role of the social worker. In R. E. Helfer & C. H. Kempe (Eds.), *The battered child* (2d ed.) Chicago: University of Chicago Press, 1974.

de Francis, V. Parents who abuse. *PTA Magazine*, November 1963.

Delsordo, J. D. Protective casework for abused children. *Children*, November–December, 213–218.

Deur, J. L., & Parke, R. D. The effects of inconsistent punishment on aggression in children. *Developmental Psychology*, 1970, *2*, 403–411.

Dion, K. K. Children's physical attractiveness and sex as determinants of adult punitiveness. *Developmental Psychology*, 1974, *10*, 772–778.

Douglas, J. W. B. Mental ability and school achievement of premature children at eight years of age. *British Medical Journal*, 1956, *1*, 1210–1214.

Elmer, E. *Children in jeopardy: a study of abused minors and their families*. Pittsburgh: University of Pittsburgh Press, 1967.

Elmer, E., & Gregg, G. S. Developmental characteristics of abused children. *Pediatrics*, 1967, *40*, 596–602.

Erlanger, H. S. Social class differences in parents' use of physical punishment. In S. K. Steinmetz & M. A. Straus (Eds.), *Violence in the family*. New York: Dodd, Mead, 1974.

Etzel, B. C., & Gewirtz, J. L. Experimental modification of caretaker-maintained high rate operant crying in a six and a twenty week old infant: extinction of crying with reinforcement of eye contact and smiling. *Journal of Experimental Child Psychology*, 1967, *5*, 303–317.

Fanaroff, A. A.; Kennell, J. H.; & Klaus, M. H. Follow-up of low birth weight infants—the predictive value of maternal visiting patterns. *Pediatrics*, 1972, *49*, 287–290.

Feinstein, H. M.; Paul, N.; & Esmiol, P. Group therapy for mothers with infanticidal impulses. *American Journal of Psychiatry*, 1964, *120*, 882–886.

Fenigstein, A., & Buss, A. H. Association and affect as determinants of displaced aggression. *Journal of Research in Personality*, 1974, *7*, 306–313.

Feshbach, N., & Feshbacn, S. The relationship between empathy and aggression in two age groups. *Developmental Psychology*, 1969, *1*, 102–107.

Festinger, L.; Schachter, S.; & Back, K. Social pressures in informal groups: a study of human factors in housing. New York: Harper, 1950.

Fleming, G. M. Cruelty to children. *British Medical Journal*, 1967, *2*, 421–422.

Fontana, V. J. Further reflections on maltreatment of children. *Pediatrics*, 1973, *51*, 780–782.

Freedman, D. A., & Freedman, N. Behavioral differences between Chinese-American and European-American newborns. *Nature*, 1969, *224*, 1227.

Freedman, J. L. The effects of population density on humans. In J. T. Fawcett (Ed.), *Psychological perspectives on population*. New York: Basic, 1973.

Galdston, R. Observations on children who have been physically abused and their parents. *American Journal of Psychiatry*, 1965, *122*, 440–443.

Galdston, R. Violence begins at home: the parent's center project for the study and prevention of child abuse. *American Academy of Child Psychiatry*, 1971, *10*, 336–350.

Garbarino, J. Some ecological correlates of child abuse: the impact of socioeconomic stress on mothers. *Child Development,* 1975, in press.

Geis, G., & Monahan, J. The social ecology of violence. In T. Lickona (Ed.), *Man and morality*. New York: Holt, Rinehart & Winston, 1975, in press.

Gelles, R. J. Child abuse as psychopathology: a sociological critique and reformulation. *American Journal of Orthopsychiatry*, 1973, *43*, 611–621.

Gerbner, G. The violence profile: some indicators of the trends in and the symbolic structure of network television drama, 1967–1970. Unpublished manuscript, Annenberg School of Communications, University of Pennsylvania, 1972.

Gil, D. G. *Violence against children: physical child abuse in the United States*. Cambridge, Mass.: Harvard University Press, 1970.

Gil, D. G. A holistic perspective on child abuse and its prevention. Paper presented at a conference on child abuse and neglect at the National Institute of Child Health and Human Development, Washington, D.C., June 1974.

Gillespie, R. W. The battered child syndrome: thermal and caustic manifestations. *Journal of Trauma*, 1965, *5*, 523–524.

Giovannoni, J. M., & Billingsley, A. Child neglect among the poor: a study of parental adequacy in families of three ethnic groups. *Child Welfare*, 1970, *49*, 196–204.

Gittelman, M. Behavior rehearsal as a technique in child treatment. *Journal of Child Psychology and Psychiatry*, 1965, *6*, 251–255.

Glazier, A. E. (Ed.), *Child abuse: a community challenge*. East Aurora, N. Y.: Henry Stewart, 1971.

Glueck, S., & Glueck, E. *Unraveling juvenile delinquency*. Cambridge, Mass.: Harvard University Press, 1950.

Goode, W. J. Force and violence in the family. *Journal of Marriage and the Family*, 1971, *33*, 624–636.

Green, A. A. Psychiatric study and treatment of abusing parents. Paper presented at the 122d annual convention of the American Medical Association, June 1973.

Greengard, J. The battered child syndrome. *American Journal of Nursing*, 1964, *64*, 98–100.

Gurin, G., & Gurin, P. Expectancy theory in the study of poverty. *Journal of Social Issues*, 1970, *26*, 83–104.

Harrison, P. *Never enough—75 years with the Children's Aid Society of Ottawa*. Ottawa: Children's Aid Society, 1968.

Hartmann, D. P. Influence of symbolically modeled instrumental aggression and pain cues on aggressive behavior. *Journal of Personality and Social Psychology*, 1969, *11*, 280–288.

Hartup, W. W. Peer interaction and social organization. In P. H. Mussen (Ed.), *Carmichael's manual of child psychology*. Vol. 2. New York: Wiley, 1970.

Hawkins, R. P.; Peterson, R. F.; Schweid, E.; & Bijou, S. W. Behavior therapy in the home: amelioration of problem parent-child relations with the parent in a therapeutic role. *Journal of Experimental Child Psychology*, 1966, *4*, 99–107.

Helfer, R. E., & Kempe, C. H. (Eds.). *The battered child*. Chicago: University of Chicago Press, 1968.

Helfer, R. E., & Kempe, C. H. (Eds.). *The battered child*. (2d ed.) Chicago: University of Chicago Press, 1974.

Helfer, R. E., & Pollock, C. B. The battered child syndrome. *Advances in Pediatrics*, 1968, *15*, 9–27.

Herrell, J. M. Use of systematic desensitization to eliminate inappropriate anger. *Proceedings of the 79th annual convention of the American Psychological Association*. Washington, D. C.: American Psychological Association, 1971.

Hersher, L.; Moore, A. U.; & Richmond, J. B. Effect of postpartum separation of mother and kid on maternal care in the domestic goat. *Science*, 1958, *128*, 1342–1343.

Johnson, B., & Morse, H. A. Injured children and their parents. *Children*, 1968, *15*, 147–152.

Johnson, S. M.; Wahl, G.; Martin, S.; & Johanssen, S. How deviant is the normal child: a behavioral analysis of the preschool child and his family. In R. D. Rubin, J. P. Brady, & J. D. Henderson, *Advances in Behavior Therapy*. Vol. *4*. New York: Academic Press, 1974.

Kaufman, I. Discussion of physical abuse of children. Presented at national conference on social welfare sponsored by Children's Division, American Humane Association, New York, June 1, 1962.

Kelley, C. *Crime in the United States—1972*. Washington, D. C.: Government Printing Office, 1973.

Kempe, C. H. Pediatric implications of the battered baby syndrome. *Archives of Disease in Childhood*, 1971, *46*, 28–37.

Kempe, C. H. A practical approach to the protection of the abused child and rehabilitation of the abusing parent. *Pediatrics*, 1973, *51* (Pt. 3), 804–812.

Kempe, C. H., & Helfer, R. E. *Helping the battered child and his family*. Lippincott, 1972.

Kempe, C. H.; Silverman, F. N.; Steele, B. B.; Droegemueller, W.; & Silver, H. K. The battered-child syndrome. *Journal of the American Medical Association*, 1962, *181*, 17–24.

Kennell, J. H.; Gordon, D.; & Klaus, N. H. The effect of early mother-infant separation on later maternal performance. *Pediatric Research*, 1970. (Abstract 150)

Klaus, M. H., & Fanaroff, A. A. *Care of the high-risk neonate*. Philadelphia: Saunders, 1973.

Klein, M., & Stern, L. Low birth weight and the battered child syndrome. *American Journal of Diseases of Childhood*, 1971, *122*, 15–18.

Korner, A. F. The effect of the infant's state, level of arousal and ontogenetic stage on the caregiver. In M. Lewis and L. A. Rosenblum (Eds.), *The effect of the infant on its caregiver*. New York: Wiley, 1974.

Korsch, B.; Christian, J.; Gozzi, E.; & Carlson, P. Infant care and punishment: a pilot study. *American Journal of Public Health*, 1965, *55*, 1880–1888.

Kosol, H.; Boucher, R.; & Garofolo, R. The diagnosis and treatment of dangerousness. *Crime and Delinquency*, 1972, *18*, 371–393.

Laupus, W. E. Child abuse and the physician. *Virginia Medical Monthly*, 1966, *93*(1), 1–2.

Laury, G. V. The battered child syndrome: parental motivation, clinical aspects. *Bulletin of New York Academy of Medicine*, 1970, *46*, 676–685.

Lawrence, J. E. S. Science and sentiment: overview of research on crowding and human behavior. *Psychological Bulletin*, 1974, *81*, 712–720.

Leifer, A. D., Leiderman, P. H., & Barnett, C. R. Mother-infant separation: affects on later maternal behavior. Unpublished manuscript, Stanford University, 1970.

Leifer, A. D.; Leiderman, P. H.; Barnett, C. R.; & Williams, J. A. Effects of mother-infant separation on maternal attachment behavior. *Child Development*, 1972, *43*, 1203–1218.

Lenoski, E. F. Translating injury data into preventive and health care services—physical child abuse. Unpublished manuscript, University of South California School of Medicine, Los Angeles, 1974.

Levy, R. I. On getting angry in the Society Islands. In W. Caudill & T. Y. Lin (Eds.), *Mental health research in Asia and the Pacific*. Honolulu: East-West Center Press, 1969.

Lezine, I. The psychomotor development of young prematures. *Etudes Neo-Natales*, 1958, *7*, 1–50.

Liebert, R. M.; Neale, J. M.; & Davidson, E. S. *The early window: effects of television on child and youth*. New York: Pergamon, 1973.

Light, R. Abuse and neglected children in America: a study of alternative policies. *Harvard Educational Review*, 1973, *43*, 556–598.

Loew, C. A. Acquisition of a hostile attitude and its relationship to aggressive behavior. *Journal of Personality and Social Psychology*, 1967, *5*, 335–341.

Loo, C. M. The effects of spatial density on the social behavior of children. *Journal of Applied Social Psychology*, 1972, *2*, 372–381.

McCord, W.; McCord, J.; & Howard, A. Familial correlates of aggression in nondelinquent male children. *Journal of Abnormal and Social Psychology*, 1961, *62*, 79–93.

McFall, R. M., & Twentyman, C. T. Four experiments on the relative contribution of rehearsal, modeling, and coaching to assertion training. *Journal of Abnormal Psychology*, 1972, *61*, 199–218.

McFerran, J. Parents' groups in protective services. *Children*, 1958, *5*, 223–228.

McKinley, D. G. *Social class and family life*. New York: Free Press, 1964.

Mahoney, M. J. A residential program in behavior modification. Paper presented at the fifth annual meeting of the Association for the Advancement of Behavior Therapy, Washington, D. C., September 1971.

Mead, M. *Sex and temperament in three savage tribes*. New York: Morrow, 1935.

Melnick, B., & Hurley, J. Distinctive personality attributes of child-abusing mothers. *Journal of Consulting and Clinical Psychology*, 1969, *33*, 746–749.

Merril, E. J. *Protecting the battered child*. Denver: Children's Division, American Humane Association, 1962.

Milgram, S. *Obedience to authority*. New York: Harper & Row, 1974.

Miller, D. S. Fractures among children. *Minnesota Medicine*, 1959, *42*, 1209–1213.

Milow, I., & Lourie, R. The child's role in the battered child syndrome. *Society for Pediatric Research*, 1964, *65*, 1079–1081.

Mischel, W. *Personality and assessment*. New York: Wiley, 1968.

Mischel, W. Toward a cognitive social learning reconceptualization of personality. *Psychological Review*, 1973, *80*, 252–283.

Mitchell, R. E. Some social implications of high density housing. *American Sociological Review*, 1971, *36*, 18–29.

Monahan, J. The prediction and prevention of violence. Proceedings of the Pacific Northwest Conference on Violence and Criminal Justice. Issaquah, Wash., 1973.

Moore, J. L., Jr., Reporting of child abuse. *Journal of the Medical Association of Georgia*, 1966, *55*, 328–329.

Moorehead, C. Seven-man team helps parents of battered babies. *Times Educational Supplement*, 1970, *12*, 2897.

Mulvihill, D. J., & Tumin, M. M. Crimes of violence. *Staff report to the National Commission on the Causes and Prevention of Violence*. Washington, D.C.: Government Printing Office, 1969.

National Center for the Prevention and Treatment of Child Abuse and Neglect. *National Child Protection Newsletter*, 1973, *1*, 1–3.

Newson, J., & Newson, E. Four years old in an urban community Chicago: Aldine, 1968.

Niem, T. C., & Collard, R. Parental discipline of aggressive behaviors in four year old Chinese and American children. Paper presented at the annual meeting of the American Psychological Association, Washington, D.C., 1971.

Nurse, S. M. Familial patterns of parents who abuse their children. *Smith College Studies in Social Work*, 1964, *35*, 11–25.

O'Brien, T. E. Violence in divorce-prone families. *Journal of Marriage and the Family*, 1971, *33*, 292–298.

O'Conner, R. D. Modification of social withdrawal through symbolic modeling. *Journal of Applied Behavior Analysis*, 1969, *2*, 15–22.

Osofsky, J. D., & Danzger, B. Relationships between neonatal characteristics and mother-infant interaction. *Developmental Psychology*, 1974, *10*, 124–130.

Palmer, S. *The violent society*. New Haven, Conn.: College and University Press, 1972.

Parents Anonymous, Inc. Procedures and concepts manual. Redondo Beach, Calif.: National Parent Chapter, 1972.

Parke, R. D. Effectiveness of punishment as an interaction of intensity, timing, agent nurturance, and cognitive structuring. *Child Development*, 1969, *40*, 213–235.

Parke, R. D. The role of punishment in the socialization process. In R. A. Hoppe, G. A. Milton, & E. C. Simmel (Eds.), *Early experiences and the processes of socialization*. New York: Academic Press, 1970.

Parke, R. D. Some effects of punishment on children's behavior. In W. W. Hartup (Ed.), *The young child*. Vol. 2. Washington, D.C.: National Association for the Education of Young Children, 1972.

Parke, R. D. Rules, roles and resistance to deviation in children: explorations in punishment, discipline and self control. In A. Pick (Ed.), *Minnesota symposia on child psychology*. Vol. *8*. Minneapolis: University of Minnesota Press, 1974.

Parke, R. D., & Deur, J. L. Schedule of punishment and inhibition of aggression in children. *Developmental Psychology*, 1972, *7*, 266–269.

Parke, R. D., Ewall, W., & Slaby, R. G. Hostile and helpful verbalizations as regulators of nonverbal aggression. *Journal of Personality and Social Psychology*, 1972, *23*, 243–248.

Parke, R. D., & O'Leary, S. Family interaction in the newborn period: some findings, some observations, and some unresolved issues. In K. Riegel & J. Meacham (Eds.), *The developing individual in a changing world*. Vol. *2*. *Social and environmental issues*. The Hague: Mouton, 1975.

Parke, R. D., Sawin, D. B., & Kreling, B. The effect of child feedback on adult disciplinary choices. Unpublished manuscript, Fels Research Institute, 1974.

Parmalee, A. H., Jr. Development of states in infants. In C. Clemente, D. Purpurpa, & F. Mayer (Eds.), *Maturation of brain mechanisms related to sleep behavior*. New York: Academic Press, 1972.

Patterson, G. R. Interventions for boys with conduct problems: multiple settings, treatments and criteria. *Journal of Consulting and Clinical Psychology*, 1974, *42*, 471–481.

Patterson, G. R., & Cobb, J. A. A dyadic analysis of "aggressive" behavior. In J. P. Hill (Ed.), *Minnesota symposia on child psychology*. Vol. *5*. Minneapolis: University of Minnesota Press, 1971.

Patterson, G. R., & Cobb, J. A. Stimulus control for classes of noxious behavior. In J. S. Knutson (Ed.), *The control of aggression: implications from basic research*. Chicago: Aldine, 1973.

Patterson, G. R., & Gullion, M. E. *Living with children*. Champaign, Ill.: Research Press,

1968.

Patterson, G. R., & Reid, J. B. Reciprocity and coercion: two facets of social systems. In C. Newunger & J. Michael (Eds.), *Behavior modification in clinical psychology*. New York: Appleton-Century-Crofts, 1970.

Paulson, M., & Blake, P. The physically abused child: a focus on prevention. *Child Welfare*, 1969, *48*, 86–95.

Paulson, M. J., & Chaleff, A. Parent surrogate roles: a dynamic concept in understanding and treating abusive parents. *Journal of Clinical Child Psychology*, 1973, *2*, 38–40.

Pike, E. L. C.A.L.M.: A timely experiment in the prevention of child abuse. *Journal of Clinical Child Psychology*, 1973, *2*, 43–45.

Pinkney, A. *The American way of violence*. New York: Random House, 1972.

Platou, R. V.; Lennox, R.; & Beasley, J. D. Battering. *Bulletin of the Tulane Medical Faculty*, 1964, *23*, 157–165.

Pollock, D., & Steele, B. A therapeutic approach to the parents. In C. H. Kempe & R. E. Helfer (Eds.), *Helping the battered child and his family*. Philadelphia: Lippincott, 1972.

Rabinowitz, M. S.; Bibace, R.; & Caplan, H. Sequela of prematurity: psychological test findings. *Canadian Medical Association Journal*, 1961, *84*, 822–824.

Redd, W. H.; Morris, E. K.; & Martin, J. A. Effects of positive and negative adult-child interactions on children's preferences. *Journal of Experimental Child Psychology*, 1975, *19*, 153–164.

Rimm, D. C.; Hill, G. A.; Brown, N. N.; & Stuart, J. E. Group assertiveness training in treatment of inappropriate anger expression. *Psychological Reports*, 1974, *34*, 791–798.

Rimm, D. C., & Masters, J. C. *Behavior therapy: techniques and empirical findings*. New York: Academic Press, 1974.

Risley, T. R., & Baer, D. M. Operant behavior modification: the deliberate development of behavior. In B. M. Caldwell & H. N. Riciutti (Eds.), *Review of child development research*. Vol. *3*. Chicago: University of Chicago Press, 1973.

Robson, K. S., & Moss, H. A. Patterns and determinants of maternal attachment. *Journal of Pediatrics*, 1970, *77*, 976–985.

Roy, K. Parent's attitudes toward their children. *Journal of Home Economics*, 1950, *42*, 652–653.

Ryder, R. G. Longitudinal data relating marriage satisfaction and having a child. *Journal of Marriage and the Family*, 1973, *35*, 604–606.

Sameroff, A. J., & Chandler, M. J. Perinatal risk and the continuum of caretaking casualty. In F. D. Horowitz, E. M. Hetherington, S. Scarr-Salapatek, & G. Siegel (Eds.), *Review of child development research*. Vol. *4*. Chicago: University of Chicago Press, 1975.

Savino, A. B., & Sanders, R. W. Working with abusive parents: group therapy and home visits. *American Journal of Nursing*, 1973, *73*, 482–484.

Schaffer, H. R., & Emerson, P. E. Patterns of response to physical contact in early human development. *Journal of Child Psychology and Psychiatry*, 1964, *5*, 1–13.

Schloesser, P. The abused child. *Bulletin of Menninger Clinic*, 1964, *28*, 260.

Seashore, M. J.; Leifer, A. D.; Barnett, C. R.; & Leiderman, P. H. The effects of denial of early mother-infant interaction on maternal self-confidence. *Journal of Personality and Social Psychology*, 1973, *26*, 369–378.

Seligman, M.. E. P.; Maier, S. F.; & Solomon, R. L. Unpredictable and uncontrollable aversive events. In F. R. Brush (Ed.), *Aversive conditioning and learning*. New York: Academic Press, 1969.

Sidel, R. *Women and child care in China*. New York: Hill & Wang, 1972.

Simons, B.; Downs, E. F.; Hurster, M. M.; & Archer, M. Child abuse: epidemiological study of medically reported cases. *New York State Journal of Medicine*, 1966, *66*.

Simpson, K. The battered baby problem. *Royal Society of Health Journal*, 1967, *87*, 168–170.

Simpson, K. The battered baby problem. *South African Medical Journal*, 1968, *42*, 661–665.

Skinner, A. E., & Castle, R L. *Seventy-eight bettered children: a retrospective study*. London: National Society for the Prevention of Cruelty to Children, 1969.

Slaby, D. Program description and progress report. Children's Day School and Parent Training Programs, Department of Behavioral Sciences, Children's Orthopedic Hospital, Seattle, June 1974.

Solomon, T. History and demography of child abuse. *Pediatrics*, 1973, *51*(Pt. 2).

Spinetta, J. J., & Rigler, D. The child-abusing parent: a psychological review. *Psychological Bulletin*, 1972, *77*, 296–304.

Stark, R., & McEvoy, J. Middle class violence. *Psychology Today*, 1970, *4*, 52–65.

Steele, B. F., & Pollock, D. A psychiatric study of parents who abuse infants and small children. In R. E. Helfer & C. H. Kempe (Eds.), *The battered child*. Chicago: University of Chicago Press, 1968.

Steinmetz, S. K. Intra-familial patterns of conflict resolution: United States and Canadian comparisons. Paper presented at the annual meeting of the Society for the Study of Social Problems, Montreal, 1974. (a)

Steinmetz, S. K. Normal families and family violence: the training ground for abuse. Paper presented at Research NIH conference on child abuse and neglect, Bethesda, Md., June 1974. (b)

Steinmetz, S. K. Occupational environment in relation to physical punishment and dogmatism. In S. K. Steinmetz & M. A. Straus (Eds.), *Violence in the family*. New York: Dodd, Mead, 1974. (c).

Steinmetz, S. K., & Straus, M. A. (Eds.) *Violence in the family*. New York: Dodd, Mead, 1974.

Stevens-Long, J. The effect of behavioral context on some aspects of adults disciplinary practice and affect. *Child Development*, 1973, *44*, 476–484.

Stevenson, H. W. *Society for Research in Child Development Newsletter*, Fall 1974.

Stouwie, R. J. An experimental study of adult dominance and warmth, conflicting verbal instructions, and children's moral behavior. *Child Development*, 1972, *43*, 959–972.

Straus, M. A. Some social antecedents of physical punishment: a linkage theory interpretation. *Journal of Marriage and the Family*, 1971, *33*, 658–663.

Straus, M. A. Leveling, civility, and violence in the family. *Journal of Marriage and the Family*, 1974, *36*, 13–19.

Ten Bensel, R. W., & Raile, R. B. The battered child syndrome. *Minnesota Medicine*, 1963, *46*, 977–982.

Terr, L. C. A family study of child abuse. *American Journal of Psychiatry*, 1970, *127*, 665–671.

Tuteur, W., & Glotzer, J. Further observations on murdering mothers. *Journal of Forensic Sciences*, 1966, *2*, 373–383.

Ulrich, R. E. Pain as a cause of aggression. *American Zoologist*, 1966, *6*, 643–662.

Van Stolk, M. The battered child in Canada. Toronto: The Canadian Publishers, 1972.

Viano, E. C. Attitudes towards child abuse among American professionals. Paper presented at the biennial meeting of the International Society for Research on Aggression, Toronto, 1974.

Walters, R. H., & Parke, R. D. Social motivation, dependency and susceptibility to social influence. In L. Berkowitz (Ed.), *Advances in experimental social psychology*. New York: Academic Press, 1964.

Walters, R. H., & Parke, R. D. The influence of punishment and related disciplinary techniques on the social behavior of children: theory and empirical findings. In B. A. Maher (Ed.), *Progress in experimental personality research*, Vol. *4*. New York: Academic Press, 1967.

Wasserman, S. The abused parent of the abused child. *Children*, 1967, *14*, 175–179.

Williams, C. D. The elimination of tantrum behavior by extinction procedures. *Journal of Abnormal and Social Psychology*, 1959, *59*, 269.

Wolff, P. H. The natural history of crying and other vocalizations in early infancy. In B. M. Foss (Ed.), *Determinants of infant behavior*. Vol. *4*. New York: Wiley, 1969.

Wolfgang, M. Crime: homicide. In D. L. Sells (Ed.), *International encyclopedia of the social sciences*. Vol. *3*. New York: Macmillan, 1968.

Woolley, P. V., & Evans, W. A., Jr. Significance of skeletal lesions in infants resembling those of traumatic origin. *Journal of the American Medical Association*, 1955, *158*, 539–543.

Wright, L. The theoretical and research base for a program of early stimulation, care and training of premature infants. In J. Hellmuth (Ed.), *Exceptional infant: Studies in abnormalities*. New York: Brunner/Mazel, 1971.

Young, L. *Wednesday's children: a study of child neglect and abuse*. New York: McGraw-Hill, 1964.

Zalba, S. R. The abused child. *Social work: a typology for classification and treatment*, 1967, 70–79.

Zalba, S. R. Battered children. *Transaction*, 1971, *8*, 58–61.